Toward Self-Directed Learning in the Secondary Classroom

Toward Self-Directed Learning in the Secondary Classroom

Erik N. Powell

ROWMAN & LITTLEFIELD
Lanham • Boulder • New York • London

Published by Rowman & Littlefield
An imprint of The Rowman & Littlefield Publishing Group, Inc.
4501 Forbes Boulevard, Suite 200, Lanham, Maryland 20706
www.rowman.com

86-90 Paul Street, London EC2A 4NE, United Kingdom

Copyright © 2024 by Erik N. Powell

All rights reserved. No part of this book may be reproduced in any form or by any electronic or mechanical means, including information storage and retrieval systems, without written permission from the publisher, except by a reviewer who may quote passages in a review.

British Library Cataloguing in Publication Information Available

Library of Congress Cataloging-in-Publication Data

Names: Powell, Erik N., author.
Title: Toward self-directed learning in the secondary classroom / Erik N. Powell.
Description: Lanham, Maryland : Rowman & Littlefield, [2023] | Includes bibliographical references and index. | Summary: "Toward Self-Directed Learning in the Secondary Classroom explores the challenges high school educators face while attempting to implement self-directed learning in their classrooms. The realities of the pandemic and post-pandemic protocols have created new challenges that require new ways of thinking"—Provided by publisher.
Identifiers: LCCN 2023040308 (print) | LCCN 2023040309 (ebook) | ISBN 9781475873696 (cloth) | ISBN 9781475873702 (paperback) | ISBN 9781475873719 (epub)
Subjects: LCSH: Self-managed learning. | Independent study. | Individualized instruction. | High school teaching. | COVID-19 Pandemic, 2020—Influence.
Classification: LCC LB1066 .P68 2023 (print) | LCC LB1066 (ebook) | DDC 373.1102—dc23/eng/20230913
LC record available at https://lccn.loc.gov/2023040308
LC ebook record available at https://lccn.loc.gov/2023040309

*For my students,
my teachers,
my colleagues,
and especially my family.*

Contents

Acknowledgments ix

Foreword xi
Jay McTighe

1 Shifting the Trajectory 1
2 More and Less 13
3 Yeah, But . . . Now What? 27
4 The Investment 37
5 Now What? 61
6 Coda 77

References 83
Index 89
About the Author 93

Acknowledgments

I am thankful to more people than I could name in this space. That said. . . .

My students have taught me more than I have ever taught them. When people ask why I teach high school, I invite them to spend a day with me and see why I have the best job in the world. My own teachers showed me the way, especially Sue Grantham, Becky Lucke, Fred Radebaugh, Dave Morton, Jeff Halstead, Nancy Cole, Pat Pfeifer, Wayne Gilman, Bob Ridings, Susan McGinty, Mark Waldo, and Stephen Tchudi.

Several mentors have provided professional guidance along the way, for which I will always be grateful: namely, Jon Bentz, Sharon Straub, Gary Finer, and Sally Pfeifer. Foster Walsh, additionally, has been not only a professional mentor, but also a life coach and friend. The amazing people at ASCD over the years have provided me with invaluable opportunities and experiences, particularly Ann Cunningham-Morris, Jay McTighe, and the late Grant Wiggins.

The countless friends and colleagues I've met through College Board and ETS have made me a better teacher and human being, as have my amazing Gonzaga professors and cohort: much thanks and love, especially to Dan Mahoney for his belief in this project. My colleagues and friends at Ferris mean the world to me. In addition to the amazing teachers who helped with this project, I am particularly indebted to Kelly Kight, Skip and Nancy Crater, and Robin Crain.

Thank you to Rowman & Littlefield, especially Charles Harmon, April Snider, and Mark Kerr; and to Jayanthi Chander and the entire team at Deanta who made this publication possible.

Last but definitely not least, all love to my family, especially my parents, Yetta Powell and the late Bruce Powell, MD; my parents-in-law, Sheri Swafford and the late Ed Swafford; my kids, Emily, Anna, and Sam, who make me a proud and thankful dad each day; and above all my wife, Kim, who is my life, my light, my anchor, and my best friend. I love you.

Foreword

Jay McTighe

AUTHOR AND CONSULTANT

A sagacious Chinese proverb declares, "Do not educate your children as you were educated because they live in a different time." This wise aphorism certainly applies to schooling today. The world is a fundamentally different place than the one in which many readers grew up, and we are witness to noteworthy global factors that are impacting contemporary education. For example, knowledge continues to expand in virtually every field—particularly in the sciences, history, and technology—even as our time in school with students is generally fixed. Relatedly, people (including youngsters) can now access much of the world's information on a handheld device. New technologies, such as generative AI (Artificial Intelligence), promise to be both disruptive and transformative in all facets of life, including education. These changes are occurring even as humanity faces existential challenges brought on by the effects of climate change, global migration patterns, and new diseases that continue to emerge and mutate.

Factors such as these are causing educators to question what "content" should be taught explicitly, what can be located when needed, and what skills deserve greater priority. There is a growing recognition that an education that continues to simply impart known knowledge in a traditional manner is unlikely to fully prepare today's students for a rapidly changing, unpredictable world.

It is within this context that Dr. Powell's book offers a timely and relevant contribution to the field. He makes the case that a contemporary education should place a premium on the development of learners capable of self-direction and become increasingly able to autonomously navigate their own learning, within and beyond the school walls.

Powell's argument for the virtues of self-directed learning is not a new one, and he documents historical calls for this outcome as part of an overall educational mission. However, the book's greatest strength lies not so much in its research into the historical record, but in its practical prescriptions for the present. Indeed, Powell speaks in a practitioner's voice to share the wisdom derived from thirty years of personal experiences in his classroom. He presents strategies needed to support and sustain self-directed learning, and his views are validated and amplified by his teaching colleagues who contributed to the "action research" findings he describes.

Readers of this book will come to know a dedicated veteran teacher who is committed to cultivating self-directed learners. His credibility comes not only from the specific methods that have worked for him and his students, but also his willingness to confront the systemic factors (e.g., content "coverage" demands and standardized test pressures) and "yes, but . . ." objections that can derail well-intentioned efforts to build autonomous learners.

You have no doubt chosen this book because you value self-directed learning. I trust that you will gain both motivation and practical ideas for cultivating these enduring skills in the learners you serve. Your students will appreciate and thank you for your efforts—if not immediately, then when they realize the value of applying their self-direction skills to future learnings in their careers and throughout their lives.

Chapter 1

Shifting the Trajectory

"Just before dawn one winter's morning," opens the novel, "New Year's Day or thereabouts, two real, full-grown, living men fell from a great height, twenty-nine thousand and two feet, towards the English Channel, without benefit of parachutes or wings, out of a clear sky" (Rushdie, 1988, p. 3). Both the abruptness and absurdity of this scene do more than simply catch the attention of readers; they signal a surreal, complex, trajectory-shifting moment in the expectations of the readers as well as, clearly, the characters who started their flight in one direction and saw it change significantly.

How are readers supposed to believe such an insane moment—especially when the characters, Chamcha and Gibreel, survive the fall in this miraculous manifestation of magical realism—the one flapping his arms and the other clinging to him as they glide safely to the ground? And yet, there it is, as compelling as it is impossible: the opening of Salman Rushdie's complex and definitely trajectory-shifting novel *Satanic Verses*.

I cannot help but think of that opening scene whenever I reflect on the events that unfolded in mid-March 2020, when the COVID-19 pandemic shifted the trajectory of the whole world. For educators in the State of Washington, where I teach, the exact moment was March 16, the day we dismissed our students for what was supposed to be a six-week closure of campuses statewide yet resulted in nearly a year of online learning for the vast majority of students.

That moment in March of 2020 felt similar to the absurdity of Rushdie's opening scene, although it was far more real and far less magical. In an instant, the lives of billions around the globe were thrust into a new reality that would change them significantly. As a high school teacher, I felt as if my students, colleagues, and I had been unceremoniously shoved out of a plane, tossed a parachute, and told to figure it out.

"But we only have one backpack for all of us!" one can almost imagine a falling teacher calling back ridiculously to no one in particular, and hearing back, just as ridiculously:

"Yeah, I know! Just figure it out! I'm not sure what else to say," and then pausing before adding, "And don't forget to smile and make this a great experience for the students! And use the parachute! You can do this!!!"

The pandemic challenged—or more accurately, forced—educators not only to adapt to the immediate needs of students during the trajectory-shifting crisis but also to confront certain realities of education that had needed to be addressed for many years. The comforts, routines, and habits of pre-pandemic life allowed for some of those realities to remain dormant, but the pandemic produced a vivid portrayal of a system that sorely needed updates. Many teachers, for instance, realized that they could no longer teach in familiar ways and expect it to work for students. They had to rethink how to design curriculum; reconceive the scope and scale of online, pandemic education; and re-establish the very routines and habits of a professional approach some had known for decades—including, at times, ineffective practices that had settled into education at the systemic as well as the personal levels.

The fact that the pandemic caused educators to rethink their practice would not best be called a blessing in disguise—again, the image of falling through the sky seems much more accurate, and the real loss of millions around the world to the pandemic is nothing to trivialize or consider as a blessing—but it certainly destabilized our thinking about teaching in ways that needed it.

Perhaps most destabilizing to the experience for many educators was the realization that the *purpose* of our work needed re-thinking. On the one hand, the essential question that had driven many teachers for years remained relevant: *What is the most effective way to help students learn*? We still sought to address that question. On the other hand, that same point of inquiry got pushed further by pandemic realities, during a time in which remote learning required unusual engagement as well as increased independence and ownership on the part of students to succeed. With that in mind, teachers had to ask, *what is the most effective way to develop self-directed learners*?

It turns out that it is a complex question to answer.

As the pandemic wore on, we all floundered with the question and tried to adjust to new platforms such as Zoom, Teams, and others. We tried clumsily to create some sense of educational community for our students who were being asked to function largely in independent ways. (It seemed as if, like Chamcha and Gibreel, we all landed, too—not in the English Channel, perhaps, but in some sort of nebulous body of metaphorical water that required us to turn our parachute into a cobbled-together educational raft.) We reached out for help to our colleagues through texts, social media, and phone calls. We tried to figure it out.

During those interactions with colleagues, I noticed certain patterns developing, certain recurring themes emerging concerning pedagogy, purpose, and self-directedness to the extent that, in the spring of 2021, I sent surveys to nearly fifty educators across the United States at various grade levels and in different subject areas about the realities of teaching during the pandemic. I wanted to synthesize the disparate conversations we had been having to see how they morphed into patterns and themes and what those patterns and themes suggested. The responses to my survey were candid, frank, raw, and clearly revealed three concepts:

(1) Educators agreed that to succeed in helping students learn in this new reality, they had to start designing and implementing curriculum differently; (2) To help students become self-directed, educators had to invest in their students' social-emotional needs before they could expect academic achievement; and (3) All educators wanted to see their newfound practices carry into the post-COVID-19 classroom, however that might look in the future (Powell, 2021).

While the pandemic hauled these issues into the light, this was, again, not a blessing in disguise as much as it was a wake-up call or even an alert. It was also, however, not an entirely new perception. For years, researchers and theorists had sought better ways to engage students in learning that would transfer beyond the classroom walls and into the realm described variously as *authentic*, *lifelong*, *deep*, and *enduring*. Going back over the last several decades, one can see these perceptions, wake-up calls, or alerts sounding. It took the pandemic to get our attention.

Pope (2001), for instance, argued for an approach to schooling that broke free from the stressful, high-stakes, test-heavy system in place at the start of the twenty-first century and instead tapped into students' "intrinsic motivation to do well . . . to practice traditionally adult roles that lead to real consequences and skill development," rendering more authentic experiences for learners (p. 172).

Furthermore, when McTighe and Wiggins (1998) conceived of an educational framework organized around big ideas, essential questions, performance tasks, and backward design, they joined an evolving conversation that could be traced back through McLaughlin and Talbert (1993), Knowles (1975), Freire (1970), and Whitehead (1929), among others, who all sought to push formal education beyond the superficialities of rote learning and into authentic, complex understanding.

McLaughlin and Talbert (1993), for example, advocated for classrooms in which students learned "as explorers, conjecturers, and constructors of their own learning" (p. 1). Knowles (1975) called for self-directed learning in which students "take the initiative, with or without the help of others, in diagnosing their learning needs, formulating learning goals, identifying human and material resources for learning, choosing and implementing appropriate learning strategies, and evaluating learning outcomes" (p. 18).

Freire (1970) argued against the practice of students being "treated as empty vessels in which teachers 'deposit' knowledge," and instead argued for students "problem-posing" (p. 52) as active and mature learners. Decades prior, Whitehead (1929) implored his contemporaries:

> Let the main ideas which are introduced into a child's education be few and important, and let them be thrown into every combination possible. The child should make them his [sic] own and should understand their application here and now in the circumstances of his actual life. From the very beginning of his education, the child should experience the joy of discovery. (p. 2)

The ongoing quest for deeper, lifelong, self-directed learning continued with Seif (2021), who concluded that American education "is at a crossroads" and claimed that "many classrooms and schools still provide a traditional educational approach, using a model similar to one that has been around for many years" (p. 6)—an approach, in fact, that produces too few experiences of authentic learning and, unsurprisingly, little student engagement in the process.

Fullan et al. (2020) highlighted this decrease in student engagement over the last ten years and the failure of school systems to keep pace with technological advances that could help students (p. 3). Mehta and Fine (2019) declared, "teachers need to bring to the fore student thinking . . . and create a collaborative culture in which this kind of thinking can thrive" (pp. 13–14). However, their investigation of high schools around the United States revealed "gaps between aspirations and realities," in which "(m)ost classrooms [are] spaces to sit passively and listen" and "academic work [instructs] students to recall, or minimally apply, what they [have] been told" (p. 4). They concluded that many schools "are actively trying to shed the long hand of the past but have not yet arrived at the future" (p. 8). Indeed, shedding those deep-rooted, well-established beliefs, habits, and practices can prove to be incredibly difficult (Heifetz et al., 2009).

Much of that "long hand of the past" resides in textbook-based work seen as curriculum, that is, the content to be covered during the duration of the course. A certain reliability, consistency, and even comfort in that predictable stagnation makes it challenging for schools to explore new approaches. Dixon (2016), however, argued that schools must eschew the safety net of a set, textbook-based curriculum and instead build their classes for "socially connected, self-directed, inquiry-based learners" that allow students to "explore big ideas" and experience "curriculum" as a "set of powerful questions" (p. 31) that could engage students in the work of inquiry and deeper understanding.

At North-West University in South Africa, an entire research unit for self-directed learning is devoted to research and education as an imperative to move students into better positions of inquiry that prepare students to live successfully within the complex realities of today's world (Mentz, 2021). Additionally, Perkins (2020) argued for the importance of building cultures of inquiry, while Kallick and Zmuda (2017) devised concepts for helping students develop strategies for independence as learners, growing out of their work with Habits of Mind. Further, Gray (2020) and the Alliance for Self-Directed Education provided multiple resources and ideas for the importance of this approach to learning.

Despite the efforts of researchers, theorists, and innovators, though, tension persists between the emerging realization of the need to implement inquiry-based learning and the familiarity of textbook-based curriculum, sparking a series of questions—some that lead to more questions instead of concrete answers—about the nature and difficulty of the work teachers must do to create students of inquiry.

Why, for example, after decades of research and thinking about these aspects of education has practice been so slow to change? Over twenty years after the publication of *Understanding by Design* (*UbD*), McTighe continued to make the case for schools to equip "learners to face an increasingly complex, interconnected, and unpredictable world" (Seif, p. xv). What about the interworking of individual schools and educational systems, overall, has been so slow to respond to that message?

Moreover, why have so many teachers—despite their best efforts—continued to struggle to find traction in their attempts to create experiences of deeper learning? Given the number of teachers I have worked with since 1994, I am confident that it is not for a lack of effort on their part. The long nights, work-filled weekends, book studies, workshops, summer institutes, and countless trial and error have remained a constant in the experiences of nearly every teacher I have known. Are they—are we—all missing a step? Are there any easy answers to this ongoing dilemma, this omnipresent obstacle, to lifelong learning? If so, then I am sure educational writers would have solved the problem and found other matters to write about by now, and I am even more sure that classroom practices would more consistently reflect those answers.

THE AIM OF THIS BOOK

My contention in this book, therefore, is that multiple complexities exist systematically in education that problematize the efforts of educators to do what they already know they are supposed to do: that is, create strong, independent learners. The numerous how-to articles and books already in publication provide plenty of ideas and strategies for teachers to try in the classroom; however, very few address the root problems that get in the way of successful implementation. Furthermore, few of those studies come directly from the experiences of classroom teachers. Not to discredit or dismiss the efforts of researchers who work outside the class at all (including those who used to be classroom teachers), but a certain awareness and understanding comes from the immediacy of working with students and should be tapped into, highlighted, and partnered with research before hoping to move forward with any serious efforts at change—especially in the current context of pandemic and post-pandemic protocols.

My positionality, then, comes clearly from the place as a classroom teacher who is exploring this topic not only through research but also through practice—both my own and, perhaps more significantly, the practice of colleagues from different subject areas and regions who can speak directly to the challenges and obstacles that stand in the way of creating self-directed learners. I hope, more than anything, to amplify the voices of classroom practitioners not prescriptively but descriptively, trusting readers to make connections and generate comparable strategies and solutions for their own contexts.

Further, I will address the challenges and experiences primarily in secondary classrooms, and specifically high school since that is the area in which I have spent most of my teaching career. While many of the ideas and concepts in this book could apply to primary and middle-school classes, I do not feel qualified to address teachers directly at those levels with any expectation that I would be considered a credible source. My hope, though, is that a primary or middle-school educator could explore the ideas in this book in ways that could be modified and applied to their own contexts to develop skills of self-directedness in ways that are age-appropriate and lead ultimately to strong, independent people of inquiry.

The overall plan for this study, therefore, is to draw from nearly thirty years of teaching experience, current research, and interviews with colleagues both from my own learning community and other regions of the United States and Canada in order to consider how high schools might engage and guide pandemic and post-pandemic students into experiences of self-directed learning. Complex realities of today's learning contexts and ways educators work within those contexts will feature significantly in the study without offering easy answers so much as presenting situations, responses, and ideas for how to move students into positions of independence as learners who are nonetheless members of their communities.

WHAT IS SELF-DIRECTED LEARNING?

Before proceeding too far, however, it is important to clarify the definition of self-directed learning, which has taken on multiple meanings over the years and has been fused, conflated, and morphed in numerous ways according to the purposes of those applying the term. To do so, both the classic definitions of the term and more practical or applied uses of the term must be considered here.

Most contemporary researchers have turned to Knowles (1975) to provide the classic definition of the term "self-directed learning," who identified it as "a process in which individuals take the initiative, with or without the help of others, in diagnosing their learning needs, formulating learning goals." (p. 18). The narrowest sense of this description applies primarily to adult learning contexts.

Self-directed learning does not, however, limit or reduce the learning experience to isolation in which learners are completely on their own. Instead, it expands to students taking control of their learning, including the process of choosing courses, seeking mentors, and even—perhaps somewhat paradoxically—collaborating with others. People interested in any number of topics choose their course of learning, including goals, resources, and procedures (Merriam, 2017; Robinson and Persky, 2021). Educators, meanwhile, shift from primarily being disseminators of information to facilitators, coaches, designers of inquiry contexts, posers of questions, and fellow learners. They develop expertise in guiding learners.

In self-directed learning, motivation resides not solely in, or even primarily in, an external but rather an internal source to drive exploration of and develop proficiency in and understanding of subjects with various degrees of external guidance as needed. In the simplest sense of the term, self-directed learning is about individuals navigating their own learning experiences as part of a larger learning community.

SELF-DIRECTED LEARNING BY ANY OTHER NAME

As more educational researchers have worked with the ideas of Knowles, however, they have applied the terminology of self-directed learning to fit their respective fields and nuanced circumstances. For example, in a recent literature review, Brandt (2020) clarified, "Different fields of study take different perspectives and use different terminology when defining, delineating, and measuring these skills, which can cause confusion across related terms and definitions" (p. 5). Whether researchers use terms such as self-directed learning, personalized learning, deep learning, lifelong learning, or some related nomenclature, the processes described are similar and, in many ways, synonymous, and so offer more resources to consider and work with when researching ways to develop students of inquiry. Nearly every researcher contextually defines this process for their own work.

For instance, in a constructivist research study involving twelve education students at a South African university, Du Toit-Brits (2019) adhered to the term self-directed learning and directly conceptualized its meaning "as a process mediated by the interaction between the student and the learning environment, where educators and their expectations of students play an important role in guiding students towards self-directedness" (p. 2). While self-directedness resides as the goal, in this context Du Toit-Brits clarified a role for educators as well, primarily as a guide or coach of the learner.

Tan (2018) further examined the role teachers play in developing self-directed learners by exploring connections with Freirean and Confucian thought in which educators play active roles in designing learning experiences, guiding students, and even partnering with them as fellow learners. For Tan, Freire's dialogic, "problem-posing" approach leads to inquiry and ultimately humanization in which students, working with peers and teachers who have expertise in content as well as learning strategies, explore the world to uncover layers of oppression and transform reality to improve their lives and communities (p. 464). Without teachers, this level of inquiry is extremely difficult to attain.

Tan framed this attainment of humanization in terms of two Confucian concepts: *ren* and *junzi*. According to Tan, *ren* is the "attainment of humanity or benevolence" for people, "the overarching and general quality that encompasses all virtues such as respect, sincerity, empathy, courage, strength, decisiveness, simplicity, tolerance, trustworthiness, diligence, and generosity" (p. 465). Moreover, a *junzi* is "an autonomous and empowered person who leads and influences others to live morally in accordance with the Confucian normative tradition" (p.467). The attainment of *ren* and *junzi*, therefore, requires the guidance of others to help them along the way: namely, teachers. Strong, critical, independent learners who know how to follow their own intellectual interests and how, in turn, to guide others do not develop in a vacuum. They grow as a result of their social interactions and inquiries that make them into stronger people who understand how to make better decisions for their own learning and address the ramifications those decisions have on their communities.

Pane et al. (2017) adapted the term personalized learning in a report funded by the Gates Foundation to describe a similar process: namely, an educational approach "to be driven largely by the individual student's needs, interests, and context; and to be informed by ongoing conversations with the student and the adults in his or her life" (p. 2). While some of the descriptions in this report might fall short of the Confucian ideals of *ren*, they nonetheless point toward developing strong, critical learners who develop with the help of others. Here, both the "classic" definition of self-directed learning and Pane's description of personalized learning put students in the driver's seat for much of their learning experience with the intent of cultivating independence, learning interests, and processes.

Similarly, a summary report by Microsoft (2020) called for a re-shaping of the educational system in the United States that fosters "greater student-centricity and a heightened focus on learners" who "navigate their own learning" to "explore and make choices that unlock their curiosity and potential" (p. 4). While a corporate report in a primarily academic work might raise concerns among some readers, the report's findings represent those of another key stakeholder to see how self-directed learning as a concept is used in different educational contexts and what the possible ramification of those uses are.

Microsoft's conclusion, for example, that a "personalized learning" develops deep cognitive skills and self-efficacy offers connections and considerations for any educator intent on facilitating those abilities in the classroom. Ultimately, the report cited work that advocates for placing students in positions of self-directedness. For example, by coaching students to progress in self-paced manners, educators free up learners to develop self-awareness and foster lifelong learning and capacities for problem solving. While the terminology reflects "personalized learning," the description itself invokes many of the same traits visible in Knowles' self-directed learning model.

Furthermore, the report articulated how such approaches to learning "give students more control to focus on topics that interest them, set personal goals, and motivate themselves. Student-centered instruction focuses on skills and practices that enable lifelong learning and independent problem solving" (p. 17). This aligns with the numerous descriptions of self-directed learning in other studies and stands as a functioning, synonymous definition of the term.

Another term that researchers have used to describe and define the concepts and processes involved with self-directed learning is deep learning. For example, in a research white paper written specifically to address online learning needs during the pandemic, McTighe et al. (2020) built on the framework that he and Wiggins established in earlier work (1998) to articulate a type of learning that places students firmly in the position of developing their own understanding of topics and big ideas through the open-ended exploration of inquiry-based questions. For McTighe, deep learning happens when "students come to understand important ideas and processes and are able to transfer that learning" (p. 1).

This alone does not constitute an approach to learning synonymous with self-directedness. McTighe's (2020) elaboration, however, that exploring abstract, transferrable ideas requires meaning-making and suggests the self-efficacy of learners who have taken ownership of their learning by delving deeply into highly engaging topics and thus growing in sophistication and understanding. The same qualities of "deep learning" reflect the outcomes of someone who has participated in "self-directedness." His recent work on self-directed learning, moreover, strengthens the connections between the two concepts (McTighe and Tucker, 2022).

Mehta and Fine (2019) added further insight into the concept of deep learning during their observations in over thirty schools across the country reputed for being "high achieving." Their use of the term "deeper meaning," which they described as "an umbrella term . . . to encompass a range of desirable attributes of schooling" (p. 10), comes primarily from the Hewlett Foundation's definition of schools that help learners "develop significant understanding of core academic content, exhibit critical thinking and problem-solving skills, collaborate, communicate, direct their own learning, and possess an 'academic mindset'" (p. 10). While this entails a variety of academic and intellectual experiences, self-directedness—that is, when students "direct their own learning"—comes through clearly among them.

Later in their study, Mehta and Fine (2019) developed their understanding of the concept by describing learning experiences that were driven and developed by students in contextualized content areas (p. 225). Students, in fact, were entrusted with more responsibility for their learning in a course of "self-directed study" (p. 227). Mehta and Fine further observed this learning in a class wherein the teacher "created an environment in which students could drive their own learning" (p. 228), reinforcing the notion that the different terms researchers have used all aim for the same independence, efficacy, and inquiry at the heart of effective educational practices.

Furthermore, Seif (2020) used the umbrella term "lifelong learning" to describe multiple, complex, inquiry-based practices such as to "prepare students to adapt to societal changes" (p. 5). Seif extended this definition to convey the idea that lifelong learning is necessary "to focus on developing . . . a complex knowledge base, critical skills, growth mindset, and the ability to learn and problem solve independently and interdependently" (p. 6).

Some of the specific terminologies differ; however, the principles, processes, and goals are largely synonymous and helpful toward building a working definition of the concept of self-directed learning and what it can look like in a contemporary context. I am not convinced that one term offers essential advantages over any of the others. For the purpose of this study, I choose self-directed because I think it aligns most accurately with some of the foundational concepts articulated by Knowles, along with the way others have built on that foundation, and captures the idea of how we would like learners to develop—that is, into strong, independent people of inquiry—amid the trajectory-shifting complexities of life in the twenty-first century.

SUMMARY

The COVID-19 pandemic forced many educators into hard conversations about their practice and purpose in the classroom to help students become better learners, and specifically self-directed learners. While the concept of self-directed learning has been around and applied in different ways for several decades, it has found inconsistent success due to a range of complex factors. By exploring the complexities educators face in contemporary high schools within the context of contemporary research and interviews, this book will consider how teachers, despite the many challenges that exist, may design and implement self-directed learning experiences for their students.

Chapter 2

More and Less

Among the many levels of complexity existent in today's secondary schools are the problematic structures of past practices with current needs. For the most part, schools in the United States continue to operate according to the Carnegie Unit model configured well over a hundred years ago that seems more conducive to factory work than communities of inquiry, reflection, and growth. Multiple periods per day driven at times by highly structured learning targets, state mandates, and high-stakes tests have become the norm systemically. Those who have worked in environments different from that tend to be the exception rather than the norm, and most educators will encounter that regimentation at one point or another during their career (Pope, 2001; Dixon, 2016).

Within that structure, teachers must nonetheless find ways to engage students who enter their classes with a range of complex needs—socially, emotionally, and academically complex—in meaningful work that develops certain habits and skills to succeed in their communities. Despite the driving demands of standardized tests, increasingly more expectations as caretakers for students with challenging needs, and ongoing obligations as actual content teachers, educators must capture the imaginations of their students and help them discover levels of aptitude and understanding that they perhaps did not know existed, at least not in an academic context.

Math educator and innovator Dan Meyer (2010) described the matter humorously and accurately in a TED talk when he said that, as a teacher, he sells "a product to a market that doesn't want it, but is forced by law to buy it. I mean, it's just a losing proposition." Perhaps the only description that more accurately captures the reality of a teacher's situation comes from Frank McCourt (2005), who spent thirty years as a high school teacher in the New York City public schools. He summed up a teacher's experience in this way:

I was more than a teacher. And less. In the high school classroom you are a drill sergeant, a rabbi, a shoulder to cry on, a disciplinarian, a singer, a low-level scholar, a clerk, a referee, a clown, a counselor, a dress-code enforcer, a conductor, an apologist, a philosopher, a collaborator, a tap dancer, a politician, a therapist, a fool, a traffic cop, a priest, a mother-father-brother-sister-uncle-aunt, a bookkeeper, a critic, a psychologist, the last straw. (p. 19)

Teachers play many roles in order to help students learn not just academic competencies but also life skills, and they must do so within structures and circumstances that are not always conducive to deep, rich learning. They must, however, find ways to do so, anyway.

The case of my Lyft driver, for instance, speaks volumes about the situation of many teachers in the United States. Recently, my wife, son, and I were in Memphis, Tennessee. While taking a Lyft from our hotel to downtown, we engaged in the typical small talk with our driver. Before too long, it came out that both my wife and I were teachers. Our driver, however, surprised us slightly when she said that she, too, was a teacher.

"Oh," I said, "that's great! Are you just finishing student teaching?"

Dumb question, it turned out. At the time, though, I figured she was a college student finishing her teaching degree and driving on the weekends to make extra money to pay for school. Or perhaps she was a first-year teacher earning a supplementary income while making the transition from college to career. After all, I recalled one first-year teacher at a school I consulted for in New York City who occasionally tended bar for that very reason.

"No," she replied, "I'm in my fifth year of teaching."

My wife and I were a little confused. Why would a teacher of five years drive a Lyft? Doing so seemed to go beyond desiring extra spending cash. Didn't she need her weekends to rest, grade, and plan (not necessarily in that order)? I tried to ask that rather indelicate question in the most delicate manner possible.

She probably wondered what planet we came from where teachers did not have to work two jobs. As she explained to us, many teachers she knew had to work two jobs to make ends meet (Will, 2018). Needless to say, I was dumbfounded. How could a fifth-year teacher, someone still learning the craft of teaching but clearly invested in the profession, be expected to do her best work with students while also needing to work a second job? What kind of structure was in place that forced educators to do that? When would she have time to rest, plan, and grade—again, not necessarily in that order—to be at her best for students if she had to work a second job?

Not surprisingly, she confessed to being on the verge of leaving education in order to make a better living. My heart broke when I heard this, just like it does each time I hear similar stories from young teachers around the country. When one of my former students, for example, who was developing into an excellent teacher in Massachusetts, told me he was leaving the profession to start his own business—as a dog walker in Boston—because he could make more money doing that than he could by teaching, my blood boiled. And when my daughter moved back to Washington after two years of teaching in Idaho and thought her first paycheck as a teacher in this state was a mistake because she was making significantly more money than she had been making, I thought, no wonder young teachers around the country are leaving the profession so quickly.

These stories are not intended to solve the issue of remuneration for teachers in many (most?) of the states across this country, but they do reflect the unfavorable circumstances and structures that many educators encounter while entering and trying to establish themselves in the profession. How can these teachers be expected to create rich, meaningful learning experiences for their students when they can't even afford to pay their own bills on their salaries and must take on second jobs—some of which turn out to be more rewarding, if not emotionally then at least financially? (And when many students come out of college carrying significant debt, financial needs frequently beat out emotional fulfillment.) Add to those already existing challenges, the landscape-altering pandemic has only exacerbated the issues and exposed many cracks in the figurative framework of educational structures, and it all becomes quite overwhelming at times.

The notion, then, of creating learning communities of rich, deep, and self-directed learning might not seem realistic to many educators. In fact, the premise of this study might seem like a pipe dream to these teachers or to those who work in highly regimented state systems that dictate what will be taught, how it will be taught, and how it will be tested, while also restricting certain topics (Sheridan, 2022; Brown, 2022; Savransky, 2021). Within those environments, is it even realistic to talk about self-directed learning?

WHY SELF-DIRECTED LEARNING?

If, however, self-directed learning is worth it, and I clearly believe that it is based both on the research and my experiences, then I believe it is also worth trying to find ways to design and implement those opportunities for students despite the circumstances—albeit the *many* circumstances—over which I have no control.

Furthermore, if teachers play a central role in the development of self-directed learners who attain not only academic capacities but also a certain level of awareness and understanding about themselves, their learning implications, and their role in their respective communities, then they must figure out ways to engage students in those learning experiences (Tan, 2018).

Sometimes the most helpful way to think through a problem is to step outside the conventional approaches and consider new approaches that at first don't make sense. Given the current situation of many educational systems and the challenges that educators encounter daily, this might be one of those times to consider other routes to try.

I'm reminded, for instance, of the improvisational aspects of jazz, particularly as approached by Miles Davis and his frequent collaborators such as Bill Evans and Ron Carter. Davis was famous for finding ways within the structures and frameworks of musical principles to open spaces for all participants to contribute their voices in unique, meaningful ways. As Evans (1959) explained in his liner notes to the seminal album *Kind of Blue*, for example, Davis facilitated a collaborative experience in which each musician worked within the established framework of the session to nonetheless improvise in ways that are "beautifully met and solved" in their creations.

Carter, furthermore, who collaborated with Davis extensively in the 1960s in what is known as Davis's second great quintet, knew well the dynamic of community, improvisation, and thinking outside the box to problem-solve and create new experiences. As Carter explained, Davis was like the head chemist in the lab coordinating the chemicals but letting his whole team experiment as well (Schnall, 2022). Because of his willingness as a band leader to create a space for all participants to play to their strengths within an established structure, he is rightly known as one of the most important innovators in twentieth-century music.

It is not that Davis was the first to seek a balance between improvisation and structure; that was an essential component of jazz for decades. However, what Evans, Carter, and others learned from Davis was the freedom to think in different ways while maintaining balance and structure. What set Davis apart was his willingness to think differently, innovate, and see perceived misplayed notes not as mistakes or even as misplayed but rather as important steps toward creating beautiful music.

That approach to learning, experimenting, and innovating extends to others as well. Carter, for instance, has gained legendary status for his ability to design musical moments for his band while amplifying the voices of each participant. Herbie Hancock, for instance, compared Carter to an architect who is always "thinking ahead" and "building a direction" while simultaneously listening to the other musicians and what they are playing in order to build beautiful, memorable art. As Hancock said, "That's what creativity is about in jazz" (Schnall, 2022).

When it comes to the problems that face educators, then, perhaps it would be wise to consider how others such as Davis, Carter, Hancock, and other jazz musicians map their vision, plan like architects, yet encourage innovation as much as possible. While such innovative options exist for teachers, they are not always easily chosen or realized. The complex nature of implementing them in today's educational structures—which are not only sometimes outdated, under-supported, and stagnant, but also nuanced from state to state, district to district, and school to school—makes it a challenge on various levels.

Self-directed learning, therefore, provides an opportune point of consideration for how to think differently about the complex and sometimes outdated approaches to education that many of us know all too well. It's not that self-directed learning is a new concept or approach to learning in itself . . . or that other approaches, frameworks, and strategies are not worth considering as well. However, it is evident that placing students in the figurative driver's seat of their learning—while almost universally agreed upon as an overarching goal of education—has proven to be easier said than done over the years and could use a rethink or at least a consideration from a new perspective or perspectives. Just as Davis, Carter, and others dared to consider jazz in different ways by looking at new approaches, listening to each other, and altering attitudes toward composition and collaboration, perhaps teachers could similarly find new paths to innovation for their students who desperately need them today.

By drawing initially on established frameworks as well as current research and then engaging in some problem-posing regarding the challenges that make implementation easier said than done, perhaps a fresh view (if not a new view) of self-directed learning could be taken in order to give students a better chance of learning in a post-pandemic protocol and system. Perhaps more significantly than anything, a view into the realities of teachers' lives and work in the classroom could shed light on the challenges that exist and help us forge better ways to design and implement self-directed experiences for students.

ESTABLISHED FRAMEWORKS

If you have ever sat through a professional development session and wondered (privately or aloud) whether you have already done this before, then you are not alone. In fact, you are probably a teacher who has experienced several iterations of the same or similar initiative either at the district, state, or even national level. Many educational trends and fads have come and gone and will continue to do so; the discernment of educators and educational leaders is crucial to determining what to focus on and what to filter out of professional development meetings. While effective professional development with sound frameworks, materials, and goals can rejuvenate, redirect, and transform the work of learning communities, ineffective professional development can set schools back by years, cause mistrust and cynicism, and ultimately damage students and their development as learners. The stakes are high.

Teachers and teacher leaders reading this will undoubtedly have their favorite frameworks to draw on for the work of developing self-directed learning experiences. They will also avoid using their least favorites. It is not my intention here to speak badly about any particular framework. Instead, I would like to highlight a couple that have worked for me and my colleagues within the broader context of self-directed learning. If one of my favorites happens to be a reader's least favorite, then that is absolutely fine. My intention is simply to illustrate how teachers can venture into this work by developing from their current best practices rather than feeling obligated to start from scratch. Innovation—let alone professional development—does not always progress linearly. Rather, it tends to develop recursively through trial and error, repetition, revision, and incrementally building from one point to the next (and sometimes back again). The important point here is to find what is already working in one's own class and build onto it with strategies that could help their students while also keeping an open mind to learning additional strategies.

Understanding by Design

For me and many of my colleagues, *Understanding by Design* has served as a strong framework for prioritizing, planning, and implementing learning experiences for students. Its emphases on backward design, big ideas, essential questions, and authentic performance tasks all help to design work that is conducive to inquiry and deep learning. The following overview is not meant at all to be an in-depth study of the framework and its key tenets—all of which have been long established in educational circles—but rather a contextualized application and backdrop to the later exploration of self-directed learning that will be the focus of the book.

Backward Design. By starting with questions such as "What would I like my students to take away from this learning experience both in the short and long term?" and "What is so important to study about this topic?" *Understanding by Design* and its backward design approach challenges educators to begin their planning with the end in mind. There is nothing particularly novel or revolutionary about this approach per se—except for the reality that many teachers lose sight of these questions during the course of busy weeks, months, and years. Instead of having clearly defined goals for the learning they ask students to do, they tend to default to expediency, efficiency, and sometimes the easiest way to move frantic days along as smoothly as possible.

This is not an indictment of teachers who have done this. We all have. We all do. Teaching is a busy profession that pulls us in many different directions throughout a typical work day, week, and year. It is easy to lose sight of what we are doing, why we are doing it, and what we would like our students to get out of their time in our classes. Our professional reality necessitates intentional pauses to reflect on our work and prioritize the learning goals for our students. Once those goals are clear, we can begin the process of designing routes for students to achieve those goals. Backward planning—that is, determining a clear set of learning goals and then working "backward" from our goals to how we will reach them and then planning daily lessons at the end of that planning—gives teachers a better chance of setting up purposeful learning experiences for students.

If teachers and, in turn, students know where they are going with their learning and why they are doing it, then they have a much better chance of engaging in learning purposefully, meaningfully, and authentically. The route for deep learning and inquiry, and the potential for individual or self-directed learning, is in that way opened.

Big Ideas. Big ideas help educators focus their design plan by emphasizing a few key disciplinary concepts such as the American dream, problem-solving, or audience awareness (Wiggins and McTighe, p. 5). Big ideas are intentionally broad, transferable, and inquiry-based. They resist easy, rote responses and instead encourage exploration. Teachers interested in helping students find their self-directed routes would be wise to set them up with certain big ideas to explore and from which to choose, almost like choosing items from a menu, to encourage exploration and independent inquiry.

Instead of focusing on texts or coverage of material, a curriculum focused on big ideas allows educators to guide students into inquiry about those concepts central to their respective discipline and encourages problem-posing and learning marked by collaboration, exploration, and purpose.

Essential Questions. More than any other concept, essential questions might be the key to setting up self-directed learning. With their open-ended, inquiry-based, and, yes, problem-posing structure, essential questions place students into the heart of concept exploration and offer them routes to explore those concepts in highly nuanced ways. For example, if an essential question such as "How do relationships and experiences influence our decisions?" is posed at the start of a semester in literature class (or a social science class, for that matter . . . or a health class, World Language class, or family and consumer science class. . . .), then it could serve as an anchor—or, again, essential—question that not only guides the class discussions initially but also offers a recursive path for discussion and inquiry as multiple texts are studied.

Even more importantly, students may very well (and, in fact, often do) start to ask their own essential questions that branch off the original one—frequently more interesting and authentic than the original one, to be honest. Over the years, I have seen this happen time and time again when students take the initial question I have posed, work with it for a few days, and then generate their own line of inquiry that has emerged during the course of discussion, study, and analysis. By the time they are midway through their study of a particular text or unit, they have taken the reins of learning for themselves and established a new, personalized course that sets up their performance task in an authentic, personalized, and self-directed manner. Few experiences are more satisfying as a teacher than watching this happen.

Authentic Performance Tasks. The idea behind authentic performance tasks is to put students in situations that require them to demonstrate their understanding of Big Ideas, targets, and concepts by transferring their developing knowledge and skills to real-world scenarios, performances, and demonstrations. This is not to say that straightforward, traditional quizzes or exams are useless; they play strategic roles in my own classes, for sure. However, at crucial moments during a semester and year, it is important to push students beyond the traditional and typical toward the novel and contextual (Wiggins and McTighe, 2004, p. 142).

Differentiated Instruction

A natural partnership with the backward design framework of *Understanding by Design* can be found in Differentiated Instruction (Tomlinson, 1999), which aims to meet the varied needs of learners in instruction and assessment. In fact, a clear, concise articulation of that partnership was published in *Integrating Differentiated Instruction and Understanding by Design* (2006), in which Tomlinson and McTighe laid out the complementary features between the two and showed how they can be used strategically in tandem to create purposeful, deep-learning experiences that anticipate, respond to, and adjust learning processes and experiences based on the needs of the learners.

Rather than representing a strict, procedural approach to education, Differentiated Instruction aims to provide students with flexibility in terms of learning options based on their readiness, interests, and abilities. When partnered with a framework such as *UbD*, differentiation can open pathways for students to play to their strengths by choosing and, ultimately, having more ownership in their learning.

While some have criticized differentiation for not producing hard evidence of learning improvement and placing overwhelming expectations on teachers (Schmoker, 2010), I would counter that by suggesting the experiential component of placing students in the driver's seat of learning as much as possible has paid significant dividends in my own classroom over the years. Both the research and the work of classroom teachers featured in this book will reinforce this as well. Furthermore, the criticism against differentiation seems somewhat short-sighted, especially when implying that to differentiate means to plan a different lesson for every single student, every single day.

That's not how I have seen it played out successfully in classes, including my own. Additionally, the ongoing work that educational researchers and writers do with differentiation and student choice attests to its continued relevance and influence in contemporary learning communities (Skeeters et al., 2016; Martirena, 2022; Weselby, 2023).

The strategic blending of *UbD* and differentiation has proven to be an especially helpful strategy in my work as a secondary teacher. As Tomlinson and McTighe articulated, a strategic approach to prioritizing learning goals, establishing a balanced and aligned assessment package, understanding the needs of students, and planning learning experiences with those needs in mind can provide "stability of focus . . . in guiding learners to the desired ends" (pp. 35–37).

Here is how that stability and guidance could look in a classroom. Stage One of the *UbD* framework helps educators determine the desired results of their academic unit. Students, for instance, will all be expected to show proficiency in certain standards regardless of their unique circumstances. I would offer the exceptions of students with Individualized Education Plans (IEPs), whose needs are sometimes so significantly different that even in co-taught or inclusive settings, their learning goals must be different from others. That said, they can still engage in the exploration of essential questions, work on skill development according to their IEP, and experience learning that validates their place in the learning community of a general education classroom. From the beginning, then, intentional moves are made to get to know students, their needs, and devise ways to help them develop as learners.

With a fairly stabilized set of learning goals in place, educators can then determine appropriate assessment options for their students. Instead of limiting the assessment to a single test, assignment, presentation, or project, teachers plan for a range of opportunities that allow students to showcase their individual skills and interests while yet demonstrating their developing knowledge and abilities.

Sometimes these include straightforward reading checks and quizzes. Other times, especially during the primary performance task, teachers must place students in authentic contexts to demonstrate their understanding of the targeted concepts and ideas as established in Stage One. This authentic moment presents an ideal time to differentiate and open the door for students to play to their strengths and personalize their learning.

For example, an English Language Arts assessment asks students who have just finished reading Chinua Achebe's *Things Fall Apart* (1958) to explore the essential question, "How do our experiences influence our worldview?" This would be one of the questions that has guided the learning from the start of the unit. An assessment of student understanding, therefore, should not merely ask students to recall the characters and plot lines of the story. Instead, it should place students in a context to authentically explore that question.

To be truly authentic, students will need to engage with contexts that reflect their own interests and experiences. One student who loves role-playing games (RPG), for instance, might create the layout for an RPG in which players encounter similar scenarios and circumstances that the characters in the novel do. For example, early in the book, Okonkwo, the protagonist, would like to start a yam farm. Students in the RPG would face a similar challenge of establishing a farm, business, or settlement to be determined by the creativity and execution of the student designing the game. By asking players to simulate the challenges that characters in the novel face, the designer of the game is exploring the targeted essential question, digging into their understanding of it and the novel, and conceiving of ways to show their understanding in a way that reflects their interests and abilities.

Another student, however, might not have any interest in RPGs but instead loves podcasts. For them, then, the same essential question can be used as the topic of their own podcast in which they conduct interviews with the characters from the novel and show through the responses of those characters their own understanding of the question and how it is explored in the text.

A third student, meanwhile, might be a huge fan of Pearl Jam and decides to make a soundtrack to the novel using ten of their favorite Pearl Jam songs. The liner notes for their soundtrack might very well turn into an analysis connecting the songs to characters, storylines, and themes in the book all organized by the essential question.

In all of these situations, students will explore the same question and demonstrate their understanding of the novel, but they will do so in ways that are personally interesting and relevant. The combined structure of *UbD* and personalization of differentiation work together to guide students toward nuanced, authentic ways to show their understanding. And, to bring this back to the topic of self-directedness, the process allows students to venture out from the sometimes restrictive and limited assessments of the classroom and into the world of play, creativity, and personalized problem-posing and inquiry.

The fun of differentiation presents itself even more so during the stage of planning daily learning experiences and lessons for students. Once teachers have established the learning goals for the unit and determined the acceptable evidence of their assessment package—including differentiated options for students—they can plan lessons that build the knowledge and skills students will need to succeed at their assessments and demonstrate their understanding.

To accomplish this, I am not necessarily suggesting the abandonment of traditional lessons altogether. Setting the purpose for the day, activating students' thinking, and presenting materials and concepts clearly are all important. The question I would ask, however, is whether each student needs to be doing the same thing as all the others in order to explore that targeted knowledge and develop those critical skills. This is where differentiating has played a pivotal role in my own class.

While I frequently engage (or attempt to engage!) all students in the same lesson, I have also learned over the years that offering choices during a daily activity can yield significant learning returns. One of the best ways I have learned how to do this in class, especially those in which I have a high number of resistant learners, is to offer a learning menu. This particular type of differentiating, whether called a menu or choice board, has been around in various forms for years, and teachers at all levels have found ways to use them advantageously in their classes (Westphal, 2007; Bell, 2017; Learning Menus, 2018). For my students, sometimes having options for their learning activities can engage them in ways that requiring them all to do the same thing all the time won't always accomplish.

For example, in the 10th-grade English class that I co-teach with Karissa Jacobson, menus supplement our whole-group instruction. If we are exploring the question of how to create an effective argument, then we will devote whole-class time to that very question: "What does an effective argument look like?" and "How do we construct effective arguments?" We will look at examples from real life, examine a range of argumentative texts, pull examples from the texts we have already studied—including the independent reading choices students have made throughout the year—and formulate, as a class, strategies for constructing arguments.

Along the way, we will provide menus (see textbox 2.1) that allow students to pace themselves and control part of the learning in terms of when and how to learn the academic vocabulary connecting to argumentation, when to write journal entries related to the topic, and how much class time to devote to their current independent reading book.

TEXTBOX 2.1. LEARNING MENU

Learning Menu: Difficult Conversations

To what extent is it important to engage in difficult conversations? What does an effective argument look like?

Goals

Practice listening and speaking to develop communication skills
Examine and apply the elements of argumentation

Study Academic Vocabulary

Synthesis, Argument, Claim, Counterclaim, Concession, Refutation
Discord, Ensure, Eschew, Inevitable, Nonchalance, Painstaking,
Peevishness, Precarious, Quibble

Journal Entries

1. Recall a time when you attempted to persuade someone. What strategies did you use? How effective were you? Why?
2. Think about a movie in which characters must engage in difficult conversations. What strategies do they use to communicate effectively?

Grammar

Parallelism (See class resources)

Independent Reading

While continuing to read the independent novel you selected, look for moments in which characters engage in difficult conversations with others. What strategies do they use during their conversations? How effectively do they listen and speak to others? Write your questions and observations in your class notebook.

Class Reader

Select and read three texts from Unit 2 and explain how characters engage in conversations with others. What strategies do they use? How effective are they at communicating? Why?

Questions?

See or email Mrs. Jacobson (karissaj@spokaneschools.org) or Mr. Powell (erikp@spokaneschools.org).

The textbox shows an example of a learning menu designed to supplement work that our class is doing together on the topic of argumentation. The menu is set up with the essential questions of the unit as well as the learning target. By including these at the top of the menu, we hope to keep the focus on these concepts and questions and help students make connections between the work we do as a class and the supplemental work they do with these menus.

During the course of the unit, students will be able to work during designated class times at their own pace and categories to buttress the work we do as a class. For instance, if a typical fifty-minute class period is divided roughly into three sections, then one section could be devoted to menus. After an entry task designed to build community and address social-emotional completes the first section, we could then ask students to choose one option from the menu to work on for the next portion of the class (again, about a third of the time). Some students will choose to work collaboratively on vocabulary related to argumentation, quizzing each other on terms; others will work independently on their writing journals; still others will read their independent novels. The final third section of the class will be devoted to whole-group work on building an effective argumentative paragraph.

A couple of points to note in the above description. First, the allotment of time is rough and must remain flexible to meet the needs of each class. The second period may need more time with the social-emotional building than the third period does, perhaps. If so, we will take that appropriate time. While devoting a third of a class period might already raise objections from some, the reality is that investing significant social-emotional learning into class builds community, helps us get to know our students, and ultimately builds into them the skills they need to take chances, explore ideas with confidence, and develop as strong people of inquiry. That work not only addresses their very real social-emotional needs, but it also lays the groundwork for any self-directed learning they are going to do during the course of the year. The time we might initially take away from direct academic instruction more than rewards our efforts in the end if students learn to trust us, take positive risks, and grow as independent learners based on their time in our learning community.

A second point to note concerns the prompt that accompanies students' independent reading. Why does it not directly ask students to look for aspects of argumentation? This, our second menu (as indicated in the top right corner), attempts not only to address the essential questions and learning targets of the current unit but also to tie into previous learning. Given that the first menu and unit dealt with how people respond to adversity, we want students to continue looking for those moments in the text so that they build a layered, sophisticated understanding of the idea during the year. In the third menu, students will have a prompt that asks them to look for argumentation. In this way, learning builds from one concept to the next recursively and, ideally, deepens the understanding of students.

Other points to notice might include the use of a common class reader provided by the district, the email addresses for both teachers to encourage communication in as many ways as possible, and a link to one grammatical concept that students can explore on their own while also being taught it directly in class at some point during the unit.

In short, the menu provides controlled choices for students to explore and deepen their understanding of key concepts related to our whole-class work while simultaneously giving them chances to practice their autonomy as learners and people of inquiry.

SUMMARY

By strategically using established frameworks such as *UbD* and Differentiated Instruction to design meaningful learning experiences for students and incorporating specific strategies such as learning menus, we make intentional efforts with the resources we have to prepare our students and guide them into work that aims to build their capacity for self-directed learning. In some ways, the upfront work of this unit is significant and may seem daunting if one has not tried it before. At the same time, this work lays an important foundation for self-directed learning that will pay dividends for all stakeholders in the end. In that way, this design work both raises our game as instructional designers but also releases our ultimate control to students as they grow into self-directed learners.

Our work is much more and, as we release control to students, much less than delivering academic content and grading tests, indeed. It is investing in the lives of young people who desperately need—now more so than ever—adults to commit to caring enough about them to design meaningful learning experiences that address their whole lives, offer options for their readiness, and challenge them to develop as strong, independent learners.

Chapter 3

Yeah, But . . . Now What?

At this point, readers might very well have identified some of their own experiences in the anecdotes, approaches, and scenarios described so far. In fact, some might be asking, "Yeah, but what's new here? I've known this stuff for years. I've tried these things in my classes. They don't necessarily make my students self-directed." Or "Yeah, this sounds nice, but what about [fill in the blank with endless obstacles and challenges that interfere with teaching and learning]?" Such "Yeah, but" comments and questions are not to be evaded. In fact, they are real, relevant, and important points to consider when putting forth ideas about educational practice and reform. We've all posed them, and we cannot ignore them if we hope to help our students develop as strong learners.

While it is critical to consider our "Yeah, but" questions and concerns, it is also critical not to stop with them. In fact, the follow-up question—or perhaps more accurately, the companion question—to "Yeah, but [fill in the blank with endless obstacles and challenges that interfere with teaching and learning]?" is "Now what?" Educators do not have to work hard to pose the "Yeah, but" statements about pedagogy; they live with those realities all too starkly. The apathy, disengagement, drama, drugs, abuse, dysfunction, tractor-beam pull of THE PHONE, threats of gun violence, demands of high-stakes exams, and countless other distractions and pressures absolutely interfere with the ideal vision of education. The obstacles often stand like monoliths in the way of progress.

It is tempting, therefore, to raise the "Yeah, but" protests regarding self-directed learning and leave the matter to float away into the vortex of *been-there-done-that* and *this-too-shall-pass* initiatives and efforts. Regarding the topic of self-directed learning, plenty of "Yeah, but" cautions exist and must not only be asked but also be followed by "Now what?" questions that actually have viable responses. I do not believe that one, single, perfect response exists; however, I do believe that real actions and strategies must be explored and developed to help teachers find ways to design and implement real self-directed learning for their students.

YEAH, BUT . . .

One "Yeah, but" protest that someone recently posed to me had to do with the relevance of self-directed learning in today's educational climate. An anonymous reviewer for a conference session proposal I submitted asked whether this approach to learning was simply "pre-industrial" and dismissed it. While they did not qualify their meaning or understanding of "pre-industrial" or even their concept of self-directedness, their point of communication definitely indicated a "yeah, but" disposition of doubt toward the approach to learning. And while my proposal for the conference session was accepted, I do regret not being able to engage that reviewer in further discussion to hear more about their concerns. Even without qualifying their meaning of "pre-industrial"—and I do not want to assume I know what they meant—or their understanding of self-directedness, they reminded me of the important fact that mixed perceptions of the approach to learning create specific impressions that can interfere with discussions about it.

Based on the most recent research and ongoing commitment to exploring self-directed learning by scholars, educators, and research institutions, however, I can confidently assert that self-directed learning continues to have a relevant voice in today's educational climate. Having considered the "Yeah but," concern of an anonymous colleague, I need to ask, "Now what?" On the one hand, I could dismiss their dismissal of the concept and simply move on with my own work; on the other hand, I am compelled to explore their concerns further to see if others have articulated more substantiated claims about the topic in order to understand better and explore self-directedness as effectively as possible for my students.

A recent article by two scholars in The Netherlands offers such an opportunity. Servant-Miklos and Noordegraaf-Eelens (2021) concluded that self-directed learning is a Rogerian dead end and a failed venture in education that should be replaced by a transformative, Freirean-Vygotskian dialectal model. For them, the Rogerian conceptualization of self-directed learning is wholly individualistic, deriving from the belief that "the learner alone knows what is important for them to learn, since one person's reality is incommensurable with another's. The consequence is that the only valid form of education is . . . learning guided by the person's organismic valuing of his own interests and desires" and "resembles more a therapy session for educated adults than a classroom" (pp. 151–152). Teachers, therefore, play a bit part at best in this mode of learning, and students are left to do whatever seems best to them.

Instead, according to the researchers, educators should adapt the Freirean problem-posing approach to learning that sees teachers partner with students in dialectal exploration that is socially transformative (p. 155). Self-directed education will not truly empower students until it works within and through the Freirean lens.

Furthermore, Freirean problem-posing can be complemented by Vygotsky's cultural-historical psychology that believed

> All human activity was woven into a web of social, cultural and historical artefacts that it cannot escape" and, therefore, learning should reflect a "dialectical relationship between the Self and society which afforded individuals the power to transform the very social environment that was shaping them. (p. 156)

By engaging students in this process, teachers provide the field of inquiry that challenges students "to consider new information in a holistic, interdisciplinary manner" and so encourages students to develop their "worldview into a broader picture" (p. 160). Vygotsky's approach, which sees learners affirmed the role of educators in this student-centered learning by asserting their ability and necessity as more experienced learners to guide students through the dialectical process and help students think critically about their own pre-conceptions and assumptions. Doing so helps educators intentionally "tie new information, theories, and practices" into a more contextualized discussion that fosters transformation (p. 160).

The vision Servant-Miklos and Noordegraaf-Eelens offered concerning transformative learning not only provides an important critique of Rogerian learning theory but also strengthens the role of educators to guide students in the learning process. While the conclusions of their study would perhaps eschew associations with the term self-directedness, I believe there is still a path for their ideas to coincide with the approach. In fact, their ideas actually align with much contemporary literature on self-directed learning as well as the experiences of the classroom practitioners in this study.

At the same time, as this study hopes to show, many practitioners featured here would likely acknowledge the recursiveness of the problem-posing, dialectical approach that does not always yield direct results on a socially transformative level. Frequently, the process of guiding students toward self-reflection, critical thinking, and transformation is difficult and frustrating due to numerous obstacles and challenges both in and out of the class—as well as in and out of the control of the teachers charged with guiding their students along the path of inquiry. Transformation—long-term transformation—can be a slow process.

The process, in fact, can become layered with complexities and challenges from numerous sources, the least of which include students themselves who aren't necessarily receptive to the concept of self-directedness. As Wehmeyer and Zhao (2020) pointed out, "Students have been conditioned not to believe that they have the right to determine what to learn, when to learn, or how to learn" (p. 121). As a result, they might feel disorientation and anxiety when a teacher suddenly introduces the approach to their learning experience. Teachers interested in this work must not go lightly into it.

That acknowledged, teachers do not have the luxury of simply saying, "Yeah, but this work is too hard," or "Yeah, but my curriculum is too regimented to allow for this type of learning," or "Yeah, but I can't get around all the distractions and obstacles in class, especially those that have cropped up during the last few years." Those concerns are absolutely real and must be confronted. At the same time, teachers must ultimately figure out a way not only to confront those realities—some of which are incredibly daunting, prohibitive, and out of their control—but also to ask, "Now what?" Just because a lot of obstacles and challenges exist in today's educational climate—and I write this as an active, full-time teacher who poses these "Yeah, buts" in my own practice daily, weekly, and yearly—we nonetheless still must figure out ways to navigate the difficult paths toward transformation. Even with the objections and concerns raised by Servant-Miklos and Noordegraaf-Eelens—in fact, in light of their objections and concerns—I feel more compelled and even more empowered to take on the role of helping students in this process.

I am not sure whether the concerns of my anonymous conference-proposal reviewer aligned precisely with the critique of Servant-Miklos and Noordegraaf-Eelens; however, I do believe that the process of questioning, critiquing, and reflecting is crucial to inquiry and, in fact, drives it along. If we do not take the time to consider objections and concerns, then we run the risk of failing to develop our own capacity to be people of inquiry, let alone those who attempt to guide our students in that experience.

NOW WHAT?

This leads to the "Now what?" question. If secondary classrooms frequently fail to produce transformative experiences, then what are we to do about the problem(s)? The differentiated, inquiry-designed unit I modeled in chapter 2 could serve as at least a nice trail map of sorts to move students toward inquiry and self-directedness, couldn't it? (*Couldn't it?!*) Why, however, do our efforts fall short so frequently?

The following exercise is intended to push those of us who get stuck in the "Yeah, buts" toward intentionally moving into the realm of the "Now what?" by challenging practitioners to list as many hesitations, reservations, and concerns as possible concerning the idea of self-directed learning and to match each one with a corresponding "Now what?" question. For example, one very likely "Yeah, but" concern will be the constraints of time: as in, "Yeah, but, who has time to do this stuff when we are already asked to do SO many other things?" In this exercise, instead of leaving the matter at that point, one would push themselves to ask, "Now what? I know that time is limited, but I also know that developing self-directed learners is crucial to lifelong learning. What can I do despite my time constraints? What if I re-ordered how I spend each class period with my students? Is that possible?" Or something along those lines. I do not have an answer key for this exercise, but I do believe it could be valuable to help educators move themselves as quickly as possible out of the important yet frequently defeating world of "Yeah, buts" and into the arguably idealistic yet also crucial world of "Now what?"

Figure 3.1 shows an exercise for readers to explore both the obstacles and the possibilities at play when considering the goal of implementing self-directed learning in the secondary class. Try to list at least ten "Yeah, but" statements as well as ten companion "Now what?" questions that can help generate possibilities.

Readers who tried the exercise may have struggled to match every "Yeah, but" with a companion "Now what?" That is okay for now. At this point, brainstorming and considering ways to move beyond our reservations are more important than having actual answers or plans. Perhaps readers could not list ten hesitations, let alone "Now what?" questions. That is okay, too.

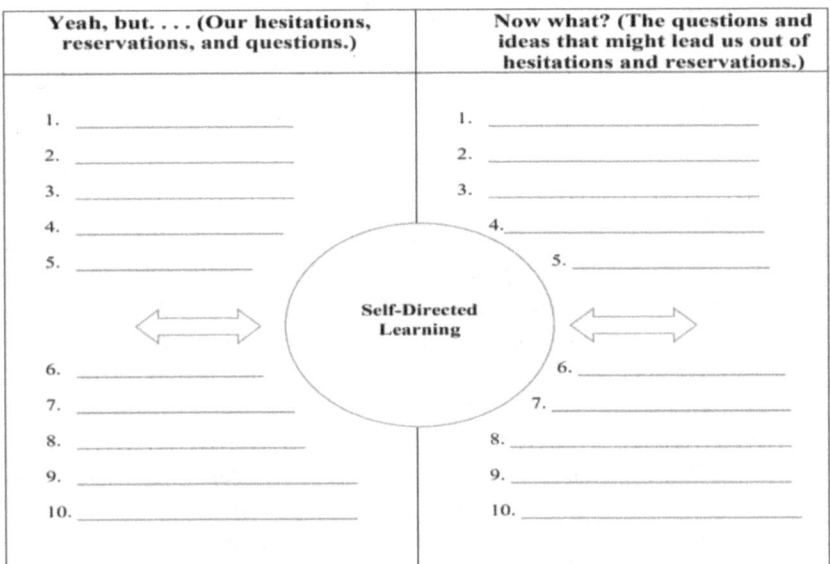

Figure 3.1. Yeah, but . . . Now What? Exercise.

Perhaps some of the reservations and "Now what?" questions and ideas seemed completely silly or unrealistic. Again, that is okay. The process itself can serve as a helpful entry point toward innovation down the road. We can't know how to think differently if we don't try to explore all the options that might inspire us.

Just as the jazz world was inspired and changed by visionaries such as Miles Davis and Ron Carter, we teachers could (and should) look specifically at educational researchers and innovators who are re-thinking and exploring self-directedness in ways that perhaps we have ignored or simply have not considered. By doing so, some of our "Yeah, buts" can lead not only to "Now what?" questions but also to specific actions that grow out of concepts we haven't considered before, or at least have not considered through fresh eyes.

For example, the Research Unit for Self-Directed Learning at North-West University in South Africa draws on insightful concepts to conceive of self-directedness that help teachers in many secondary schools re-imagine how to deal with the "Yeah, buts" and respond to the "Now what?" questions that haunt them.

With the stated mission of conducting research "to advise on ways in which learners can be assisted to take more responsibility for their own learning" (Mentz, 2021, p. 2), the Research Unit explores numerous strategies for educators to design and implement self-directed learning. Among the many insightful and helpful perspectives they explore and communicate, one particularly innovative strategy seems relevant to this current discussion. Drawing on the African principle of *ubuntu*, that is, the notion that our existence and identity are communal. In short, "I am and I exist through other human beings" (Du Toit-Brits, et al., 2021, p. 8). Rather than designing and implementing self-directed experiences that assume the universal individuality of students, this approach contextualizes people not only as learners but also as social beings who come from and work out of a collective that builds into the development of learners communally.

In some ways, *ubuntu* aligns with the Vygotskian cultural-historical dynamic as well as Freirean problem-posing. Additionally, it offers a fresh perspective, perhaps, to Western teacher practitioners with its intentionally communal vision of learning, interaction, and societal interaction. Traces of this work have appeared in cooperative learning, project-based learning, and other creative and authentic performance tasks.

However, *ubuntu* is rooted in something different altogether. Whereas many in the Rogerian and even post-Rogerian educational system would have experienced a schooling system that is ultimately individualistic in terms of work, achievement, assessment, and outcomes (including even *some* forms and applications of cooperative learning in which every learner has a specific, individual role with specific, individual aims), the *ubuntu* vision offers learning experiences that derive from togetherness, mutual respect, and the affirmation that each person is a valuable member of the community (p. 15). Accordingly, the collective work that learners do together builds community trust, responsiveness to the needs of one other, and mindfulness of joint meaning making (p.15).

What does this mean for learning, specifically self-directed learning? At first, it might seem to negate the idea of self-directedness since *ubuntu* is rooted in community and togetherness. However, given that self-directed learning involves learners pursuing their aims "with or without the help of others" (Knowles, 1975, p. 18) and given the social nature of learning, the rootedness of *ubuntu* supports self-directedness in dynamic ways that the Rogerian model arguably could not. As Du Toit-Brits et al. pointed out, the traits of self-directedness reflect those of community members more so than isolated people.

For example, drawing on the work of several researchers (Abdullah, 2001; Ertmer & Newby, 1996; Guglielmino, 2013; Lounsbury et al., 2009; Samson, 2013; Tredoux, 2012), Du Toit-Brits et al. connected several qualities of self-directedness that are decidedly social and communal, including the following:

Creativity
Communication
Flexibility
Inquiry about rules and assumptions
Embracing constructive feedback

As well as arguably more individual traits such as

Organization
Self-confidence
Time Management
Self-discipline
Responsibility
Self-reflection

among others. Learning, then, "is a joint activity and individuals form part of a larger group of people on whom they can rely, and they understand and construct information in collaboration with others" (p. 16). When approached through the communal lens of *ubuntu*, self-directed learning does not grow out of, process through, or aim toward individualist aims. Instead, it grows out of, processes through, and aims toward community enrichment and transformation. As individuals grow as members of their invested community, they become stronger thinkers and people of inquiry because of their valued place in their community and ultimately enrich not only themselves but also the community that has valued them and built them up. Thus, self-directed learning through this lens is ultimately a social and cooperative endeavor (p. 24).

So . . . now what?

If self-directed learning through the *ubuntu* lens is to happen in our own classes, what actions do we need to take regarding our current practices to build intentional learning communities in our classes? What are we currently doing to help individuals see themselves as integral and valued members of our community?

Before jumping into a plan of action, perhaps it would be wise to pause and listen to the advice of Heifetz et al. (2009), who cautioned against making changes too quickly before fully observing and diagnosing the root problems at work in a community (p. 44). Most of our practices and behaviors have developed over time and will stubbornly resist change until we have observed carefully, reflected honestly, and then planned strategically for lasting change. If we truly want to nurture our students in healthy, community-based environments in which they feel valued to see themselves as part of the whole, then we need to ask ourselves to what extent are we already doing (or not doing) that, and how we can develop that environment more effectively to help all students grow as learners.

Building on the "Yeah, But . . . Now What?" exercise in figure 3.1, the next step might very well be to pause, consider some of the "Now What?" questions, and reflect on the practical implications of those questions. For example, perhaps a "Now What?" question had to do with the use of time during class periods: "Now what? I know this work is important, but it's so time-consuming. How can I use class time differently to create intentional space to build community that leads to strong, supported learners who will grow in confidence to become self-directed?"

That's a lot to unpack.

Is it worth the effort, though? If not, then we maintain the *status quo* in our classes and hope for the best, and we shrug off future discussions about self-directed learning as "too time-consuming." Fair enough. However, if I do think it's worth the effort, then I need to pause and ask myself some hard questions about my current classroom environment.

1. To what extent is my current class time devoted to creating a collective learning community?
2. Can I identify at least three intentional practices that I engage in with students that foster a sense of community? What are they?
3. If I can't identify intentional community-building practices, then what can I identify as the predominant use of time in my classes? Am I happy with that situation?

4. Am I willing to rearrange my class time in order to build an intentional community to support the aims of self-directed learning—especially as approached through the lens of *ubuntu*? Why or why not?

Honest responses to these questions might churn deep waters in our assumptions and practices that could make us uncomfortable. We might not like our own honest reflections for multiple reasons. Maybe we will find that our long-established practices in the class have not been as efficient or purposeful as we had thought. Perhaps we will realize that to shift our practice toward intentional community building, we will need to cut into other activities; the real loss that will accompany that shift could cause some anxiety in our seemingly well-oiled machine.

Perhaps we won't be able to put our finger on one clear solution and will instead drudge up multiple factors as to why our classes play out the way they do. The shift will actually involve numerous shifts, and the reality of those shifts could be daunting to consider. Quick, "technical changes" (Heifetz et al., 2009) that deal with short-term issues by offering expedient solutions might help initially, but they might not be enough to bring about deep, long-lasting change. For instance, buying software that comes fully loaded with activities to address social-emotional needs sounds like a promising solution. In practice, however, the needs of our students might be far more complicated; giving them more screen time might not get to their core needs. In fact, for some it might just reinforce or even exacerbate the problems they are experiencing.

Addressing those deeply rooted issues in students will take a much more personal commitment and investment. The software might be one tool to use; however, it will most likely not substitute for getting to know students, listening to them, and making plans to work with them according to their various needs and interests. Such work, which reaches beyond the technical level and into the adaptive level, is far more complex and challenging. According to Heifetz, deep, adaptive challenges "typically require people to reinterpret and question their own priorities, as well as their habits of thinking and behavior" (p. 44). Are we willing to reinterpret and question our priorities and actions? Are we willing to invest in building relationships and in listening—really listening—to students? If we want to lay the groundwork for self-directed learning, then we must be willing to do so despite the unrelenting challenges that face us.

SUMMARY

The idea of building self-directed learning practices might lead some educators to raise protests or concerns that must be attended to before moving ahead with this work. Previous experiences, past failures, and persistent obstacles pose real problems for educators and cannot be ignored. At the same time, protests and concerns must be followed by solution-seeking, even if that means going outside our accustomed way of thinking or doing, and even if that departure is uncomfortable for us. If we want to institute long-term change to help our students become more self-directed, then we must be willing to take the necessary reflective and strategic steps to make it happen.

Chapter 4

The Investment

I'm fortunate to have worked with many educators who have asked the "Now what?" questions about their practices and then invested in plans to make transformative learning happen. As a consultant for the Association of Supervision and Curriculum Development (ASCD) and Jay McTighe & Associates, I have had the privilege of traveling around the country and working with schools, districts, and even statewide organizations to help educators design and implement backward design. The dedication, intelligence, and creativity of the educators I have met not only have inspired and taught me but have also helped their students in numerous and significant ways.

Additionally, my own practice and views of education have been deeply influenced by the visionary teachers I have met while serving on various committees for the College Board, especially those related to Advanced Placement English Literature and Composition, as well as exam writing for Educational Testing Services. Again, these educators have deeply invested in thinking through their practices and refining them in order to help their students learn and grow as much as possible.

It is safe to say, however, that the most influential group of educators I have met are the ones I get to work with each day in my own school. Since 1999—all but five years of my teaching career—I have collaborated, cried, laughed, and learned with teachers at Joel E. Ferris High School in Spokane, Washington. My colleagues at Ferris never fail to push me, inspire me, and help me remember my priorities when working with teenagers. They have seen me at my best as a teacher and also at my worst. They have given me honest feedback over the years on my lesson design, assessments, and ideas for professional development. They have taught me how to work more effectively with students and adults. In short, they have made me a much better teacher than I would be without them.

In this chapter, I would like to highlight some of the work these professionals have done—primarily the teachers at my school but also some of the colleagues I have met in the other contexts I mentioned above—to address the "Now what?" questions in their practices. I do not focus on them because they are perfect teachers (while I love all of them and stand in awe of them each day, they would be the first to point out their own shortcomings) but because they demonstrate consistently the reflective practices and long-term commitments necessary to bring about long-term change in their students. When it comes to the topic of self-directedness, they are in different stages of their journeys; however, they have invested in learning to the degree that they not only want to grow as educators but also do whatever they need to do to help their students become strong, independent learners.

By focusing on their work, I also hope to model and affirm what readers probably already know or at least suspect: sometimes, perhaps most of the time, the best resources for educators do not reside outside but rather inside their own learning community. When dedicated, creative, and courageous people confront the "Now what?" questions individually and even more so collectively, great things can happen. Who knows the needs of one's school better than the actual staff? Who better deal with the issues of long-term change than those who have been in the learning community and will continue to make long-term investments in that community? While occasionally an outside consultant is advisable, beneficial, and even necessary, it can be incredibly powerful for the staff of a school to draw on each other's strengths and talents to develop collective efficacy for their students.

As Friedman (2014) said, "The most powerful changes . . . are driven locally, by people who believe in themselves and who know how to get the support they need to make things happen" (p. 21). The teachers I will highlight in this chapter exhibit those traits exceptionally well and serve as examples for anyone interested in confronting the difficult realities that face educators today to forge paths for students' self-directedness.

MY LEARNING COMMUNITY IN CONTEXT

But first, some context about my learning community. As I write about it, I do so with a deep love of the school and a sense of stewardship about it. At the same time, I believe that love and stewardship both include honest reflection. By writing honestly and vulnerably, I hope to help other educators work through the issues they face in their own learning contexts. No place is perfect, and each community has its own issues and needs. If, however, people can pull together to invest mutually in a school, then important work can happen, including the mission of developing lifelong, self-directed learners.

Joel E. Ferris High School is one of five comprehensive high schools in the Spokane Public Schools system. According to the district's 2019 school profile, approximately 1,700 students from a wide range of backgrounds attend Ferris. The school opened in 1963 and has about one hundred teachers on staff, with an average experience of seventeen years (Joel E. Ferris High School Profile, 2019).

Over the years, Ferris has developed a reputation as a high-achieving, "rich-kid" school due to the number of wealthy families in the attendance area. However, Ferris enrolls students from a wide range of socioeconomic backgrounds with close to 45 percent of our population officially qualifying for free and reduced lunch (and possibly closer to 50 percent with some students not filing for one reason or another). When I first started teaching at Ferris, that number was closer to 25 percent. As our student population has shifted, we have attempted to meet those shifting needs in various ways, such as operating a food and clothing bank for many students and families. Furthermore, we run a well-established, award-winning Newcomers Center that welcomes students from all over the world who have limited-to-no English. Our staff not only teaches them the language from basic to proficient, but they also introduce them to our community and help them integrate (Rouse, 2021). While some students at Ferris drive BMWs to school, others live in dire conditions. Poverty, abuse, homelessness, and hunger are all too familiar to many Ferris students.

Furthermore, while our graduation rate is over 90 percent and we produce award-winning musicians, debaters, DECA students, thespians, and a high rate of AP scholars (Joel E. Ferris High School Profile, 2019), we also struggle with students who report feeling disengaged and disconnected from others, including adults (Ferris High School Climate Survey, 2020).

While some of the above information is useful, it is also safe to say that the pandemic turned our entire community on its head, just like it did everywhere else, and I am not sure how meaningful numbers, data, and the like are to this conversation, especially pre-pandemic numbers. Instead, I would like to focus on the people behind the numbers who come into our classrooms each day—or, in some cases, come to our campus but struggle to make it to classes. The real faces, situations, and stories of these people are the ones that matter the most to my colleagues and me when we attempt to work with them and help them become better thinkers, learners, and community members.

The landscape changed at Ferris even during the years leading up to the pandemic due to numerous complex factors in the greater community as well as philosophical shifts at the state and district levels. For instance, more typical approaches to alternative learning, such as designated alternative schools, closed and students with highly specific needs returned to their community schools. However, they did so without much infrastructure in place to support their needs. As a result, we were not prepared to deal with some of the needs of those students who returned to traditional campuses, and we experienced a couple of turbulent years.

Then the pandemic hit. As we taught from home during that year, we engaged in many conversations with each other about what we wanted and needed Ferris to look like whenever we returned to campus if we were going to optimize our efforts as a learning community. We had formal, informal, large, and private conversations with each other and did not hold back with our observations and needs.

Fortunately, our administrative team led us through the turbulence with grace, humility, and receptiveness. They supported us as well as our students and listened to our needs as well as they could. *Un*fortunately, the turbulence also took its toll on them, and several members of our administrative team either retired or needed changes of scenery by the end of the 2020–2021 school year. We were left with significant uncertainty.

Whenever a change happens at the administrative level, it can bring not only uncertainty but also anxiety to the learning community, especially when it involves the head principal who was a good man and did his best to help Ferris through challenging times. While his retirement definitely caused some anxiety, his replacement alleviated that same anxiety for many of us quickly. John O'Dell had taught at Ferris for many years and was a highly esteemed colleague when he went into administration. After serving as the principal of one of our feeder schools, he became our principal heading into the 2021–2022 school year.

John was quick to assemble an administrative team equipped to respond to the growing needs of our students and staff in the wake of the pandemic. By addressing the needs for greater mental health care and hiring additional student support staff, creating on-campus alternative learning environments, and establishing numerous sections of co-taught classes in each of the four core subjects, our administrative team observed the rapidly shifting situation, listened to the needs of students and staff alike, and acted in ways to meet those changing realities.

In many ways, the work John and his team have done reflects the research around the tripartite dynamics of social support, relational trust, and academic rigor that others have conducted over the years (Salina et al., 2016; Lee et al., 1999) in which all three components must be built intentionally attended to and implemented before schools can function and thrive optimally. Trying to navigate a staff through such work—let alone during the pandemic—has been truly challenging for our admin team, yet also admirable and inspiring.

It is within that context, then, that I would like to return to the "Now what?" question to discuss specifically the academic side of the tripartite dynamic—that is, teaching and learning—during the past several years and how, especially during the pandemic but also moving out of pandemic protocols, several colleagues at Ferris from different departments committed to reflective, innovative teaching, especially in the areas of developing inquiry. As mentioned earlier, they represent different points in the journey toward implementing self-directed learning, but they all stand as veteran teachers who have won the respect of their students, peers, and community over their careers.

Each teacher participant at Ferris, along with several educators from Canada and other regions across the United States, agreed to help me with this project by responding to a questionnaire that asked about their challenges, successes, and strategies for helping students become more self-directed. In their responses, these educators offered honest reflections and insights that reveal much about the realities of teaching high school in a pandemic and post-pandemic context. The questionnaire, aimed at collecting data primarily for qualitative analysis, provided definitions of key terms such as *self-directed learning*, *challenges*, and *obstacles* to clarify and contextualize the concepts for respondents.

For *self-directed learning*, I turned to what has stood as the standard definition of the concept since Knowles (1975) described it as "a process in which individuals take the initiative, with or without the help of others, in diagnosing their learning needs, formulating learning goals, identifying human and material resources for learning, choosing and implementing appropriate learning strategies, and evaluating learning outcomes" (p. 18).

When I asked about *challenges*, I clarified them as "those factors which present opportunities for academic, intellectual, and emotional growth and development, specifically in terms of instructional design and implementation. Different subjects, grade levels, classes, and students present unique challenges (e.g., how to differentiate lessons and assessments)."

Similar to, yet ultimately distinct from, challenges are *obstacles*, which stand as "impediments to growth and development either from internal or external factors that must be addressed in order for instructional implementation to occur (e.g., policies, extenuating circumstances, etc.)." It seemed like both challenges and obstacles deserved their own space for responses, as did successes, which participants also addressed in their answers.

Given those qualified and contextualized definitions, then, the questions participants answered were the following:

1. Based on the definition of "self-directed learning" above, have you ever attempted to design and implement a learning experience that encourages, incorporates, leads to, or constitutes self-directed learning? If not, please skip to question 4.

a. What strategies did you use to design these learning experiences?
   b. Does this experience reflect your normal approach to teaching, or was this a one-team experiment? Could you comment on the frequency with which you attempt to create these experiences for students?
   c. Did you have any success stories with this approach? Explain.
2. What challenges and obstacles stood in the way of designing and implementing self-directed learning?
3. What have you learned about yourself, your students, and your learning community while trying to design and implement self-directed learning experiences for your students?
4. If you haven't attempted to design and implement a learning experience that encourages, incorporates, leads to, or constitutes self-directed learning, what would be the reason or reasons for not doing it?
5. If you haven't attempted this type of learning experience in your class but had the opportunity to try it, would you be open to the idea?

Participants had the opportunity to include their overall reflections about their experiences at the end of the questionnaire as well. They all asked for their real names to be used.

FERRIS PARTICIPANTS

The following teachers at my school generously agreed to help me explore the topic of self-directed learning by responding to a questionnaire concerning the challenges, obstacles, and successes they have experienced while trying to design and implement this approach in their classes. While they represent a wide range of academic disciplines, they all have many years of experience not only as teachers known for their willingness to innovate but also specifically as members of our learning community. They have taught at Ferris long enough to have seen several iterations of professional development. They understand the nuances and quirks of our learning community well and can comment accordingly.

Tamara Gower. With over twenty years of teaching experience, including a Fulbright Teacher Exchange in Argentina in which she taught college students seeking endorsements to teach English as a second language, Tamara is the co-department lead for World Languages at our school. She is one of the most conscientious and intentional educators I have ever met who relentlessly seeks to design ways for her students to become active, intrinsically motivated learners. She is willing to try nearly anything to help her students invest in, take ownership of, and fall in love with the Spanish language and culture. As a department leader, she invests in her colleagues with great care and seeks their input selflessly to make sure her team is moving in the right direction for student learning.

Darci Hastings. Winner of the 2019 Washington State Science Teacher of the Year Award, Darci thrives when placing students in contexts of independent research and guiding them through their process. She has worked with Project Lead the Way for several years, during which time she has helped students place at regional, national, and international competitions. For all her work with Project Lead the Way (PLTW), however, Darci is equally passionate about helping disengaged students and has co-designed and taught a student-centered, self-paced learning lab for underclassmen to help provide a different approach to learning for them.

Karissa Jacobson. Karissa co-teaches multiple sections of tenth-grade English with me every year. Endorsed in special education, Karissa teaches courses as an adjunct instructor at Gonzaga University. She possesses an incredible ability to make every student feel like they are the most important person in the room; as a result, she breaks down barriers, builds community, and engages students in learning like few people I have ever met. She designs learning experiences that open pathways for students to grow in confidence, experience joy, and know they are valued as people. In addition to her work in the classroom, Karissa has also served as a leadership teacher, cheer coach, and class advisor.

Ashley Jones. When Ashley joined our staff in 2007, she was straight out of college. We hired her as an English teacher and the head girls' varsity soccer coach. In some ways, stepping right into a head coaching position could be daunting; Ashley, however, seemed ready for the opportunity. In fact, having just finished an outstanding college soccer career herself, she brought the immediateness of her experiences to the field. Furthermore, as the daughter of an accomplished football coach, she grew up knowing what it took to succeed in that role.

It became clear, however, that her contributions to our learning community would not only be as a coach. She quickly established herself as an innovative, open-minded teacher who sought ways to get the most out of her students. As she started her own family and transitioned out of coaching, she maintained a competitive drive to be successful in the classroom. As such, she has always been on the front line of innovation, challenging herself to learn new ways to reach her learners and put them in positions to succeed. As the English department lead, Ashley brings those same attributes to each meeting, PLC, and professional conversation. She has also served tirelessly as the senior class co-advisor, creative writing club supervisor, and project lit coordinator for our school.

James Noble. James and I joined the Ferris staff in the same year—1999. A Division I distance runner and complete history buff, James brought both his running talents and academic enthusiasm to our school and immediately made significant contributions in both areas. Having served as the girls' varsity cross-country coach for nearly twenty years, James trained a generation of athletes to develop healthy lifestyles while challenging themselves to be the best they could be. As the department lead for social studies, James consistently has modeled innovation, reflective practice, a collaborative spirit, and a commitment to doing whatever he can to help students succeed. He is one of the most selfless, committed educators I have ever worked with anywhere.

Shiho Ogata. With nearly twenty years of total teaching experience in the United States and Japan, Ogata Sensei brings a wealth of strategies, insights, and innovations to her classes each day. A proponent of the Comprehensive Input strategy, Sensei focuses on student understanding and lets production follow at a natural, steady pace. She plays with traditional seating arrangements—including the removal of desks altogether—in order to break down walls and distractions in classroom activities and to maximize participation. Students benefit greatly from the choice of learning she designs for them, the cultural opportunities she provides, and the lifelong learning and relationships she establishes with them. As the co-department lead for World Languages, she facilitates her part of department meetings and professional development with care, humor, and purpose.

Tom Rye. In 2001, Tom joined the Ferris faculty and immediately established himself as a leader. An unbelievably strategic thinker, Tom is consistently ten steps ahead of everyone else. Winner of a Christa McAuliffe Excellence in Teacher Education Award in 2000, Tom was one of the first in Washington State to become National Board Certified. Early in his career, he guided his middle schoolers to design and present more efficient mail routes to the local post office. The designs were so well thought-out and articulated that the post office changed one of their routes to reflect the plans of Tom's students.

Tom has taught as an adjunct instructor at Gonzaga University and, as a consultant for both ASCD and McTighe & Associates, has delivered professional development for schools and districts around the United States. He has written an online curriculum, been featured in instructional videos, and led both his department and district through several important initiatives in math education. He brings a passion, purpose, and expertise to campus each day that is simply unparalleled.

Emily Torres. Emily might very well be the Platonic ideal of the teacher who cares deeply for students and gives selflessly for their well-being. An award-winning teacher who has taught multiple levels of English at Ferris for over twenty years, Emily has also served as coach of the dance team, senior class co-advisor, and surrogate mom to every student who has walked into her class. She is incredibly strategic, smart, funny, and compassionate.

While she could teach any level of English, she is particularly passionate about helping students who have been affected by trauma. In fact, she has taken that passion and designed an entire course around the subject, having completed training for trauma-based instruction and delivered professional development on the subject. Partnering with other teachers and community members such as clinical psychologists, Emily exemplifies the idea of addressing social-emotional needs and teaching the whole child.

Shared Qualities

Again, these teachers would be the first to point out their own faults in the classroom. Further, while I could have included any number of other colleagues from Ferris over the years I have taught there, these colleagues have consistently demonstrated intentional efforts to move students into the driver's seat of their learning. Their willingness to help me with this exploration of self-directedness corresponds with their professional values and practices about teaching and learning.

My guess is that readers will recognize teachers and colleagues who demonstrate the same or similar attributes: namely, thinking purposefully and strategically about instructional design; committing to teaching the whole child, even when—or, especially when, perhaps—that work becomes glaringly messy and inconvenient to the smooth order of classroom routines; and understanding that the work of teachers is to develop students into strong, independent, self-directed learners . . . and be willing to try to make that happen.

In many ways, these teachers demonstrate the qualities Mehta and Fine (2019) observed in high schools around the United States who had experienced success in placing students in positions to develop their own learning. Even as the researchers found many schools lacking in that aim—including schools reputed to be innovative and high achieving—they did find several with teachers who seemed to answer the call of nurturing academic learning with a true spirit of inquiry and providing the support necessary to pursue their interests.

Many of those teachers, however, taught elective courses that tended naturally toward student interest and choice. When students had choices to take elective courses, they were demonstrating initiative, taking the wheel of education, and functioning to some degree with self-directedness. Performative electives such as music, for instance, build intrinsically from and toward student interest, initiative, and outcome. Moreover, even core electives seemed more frequently to offer students routes for choice and self-directedness. This presented new opportunities, as well as challenges, for students not used to learning in this way. Having to be "more responsible, more in charge of their own learning," provided opportunities for inquiry and growth; however, it also presented challenges to students who were not used to "a course of self-directed study," particularly in terms of motivation and organization (p. 227).

Mehta and Fine saw this type of learning, what they call "deep learning," occasionally. They concluded, however, that it needed to happen more frequently and consistently if schools, both individually and systemically, would experience long-term change. After all their travels, interviews, and observations, their conclusion on the matter struck me as most curious and appealing. Despite the many different types of schools they visited with numerous special programs and approaches in place to foster deep learning, they found a common denominator among them: "having adults who really cared about their students, who knew when to push and when to support, was critical to the success of all the good schools that we encountered" (p. 378). That, more than anything else, describes the colleagues who helped me with this study.

NON-FERRIS PARTICIPANTS

While most of the help I received for this project came from my colleagues at Ferris, I did seek additional input from several colleagues around the United States and Canada to provide further perspective and insight. I don't pretend that this is a comprehensive study at all or that the views of my colleagues in other learning communities reflect all teachers in their respective regions or even schools; at the same time, I believe they added invaluable ideas and strategies to complement the ethnography at my own school.

Ryan Feehan and **Brad Koshka** both work as secondary administrators in Edmonton, Alberta. Ryan, an educator of over fifteen years, and Brad, an educator with thirty-five years of experience, have served in leadership roles while establishing self-directed learning programs in their learning communities. They both place a premium on relationships with students and build specific, intentional structures in order to ensure the implementation of self-directed learning experiences happened at their schools.

Adam Galvez. With teaching experience in the Northwest, Southwest, and Midwest, Adam has experienced three distinct educational contexts during his career. He currently teaches theology at a Catholic school in Chicago and aims to foster a learning environment of inquiry and collaboration. He has had a great deal of coaching experience as well.

Enithie Hunter. Enithie brings a wealth of experience to this study. Having taught in both public and private schools in Georgia, Panama, and New Jersey, she currently teaches at a boarding school. Moreover, Enithie has been deeply involved in the AP program, serving as both an exam reader and, most recently, as co-chair of the Development Committee for English Literature and Composition as well as a Question Leader during the annual exam reading. She is a proponent of the Harkness Approach to learning, which focuses on discussion-based inquiry in which teachers function more as facilitators than lecturers.

Dr. Minaz Jooma. With over thirty-five years of teaching experience, Dr. Jooma stands out to me as one of the very best in the profession for her insights, methods, intelligence, and kindness. Currently at a high-achieving high school in New Jersey, Dr. Jooma brings as much passion for learning to the class and belief in her students as she does her immense content knowledge of literature, particularly British literature. In addition to teaching, she has extensive experience working with the College Board on the AP exam. As a former co-chair of the English Literature and Composition Committee, she brings insights to the course, exam, and methodology like few people I have ever met.

Again, though, what truly stands out to me is her passion for learning and helping students. In nearly every conversation she and I have concerning teaching, we tend to drift ultimately toward how to help students, especially with the shifting landscape of contemporary education and the very real needs that accompany those shifts.

Jim Wickes. Jim is an experienced educator of over twenty years who has recently transitioned from the classroom into administration. With a wealth of experience as an AP English teacher, Jim has participated in the annual AP Reading multiple times and worked as an AP mentor. He lives and works in Georgia, where he is also a long-time soccer coach.

DATA COLLECTION AND ANALYSIS

All of the participants offered candid, reflective responses to the questions that helped create a picture of the many obstacles, challenges, and successes they had experienced in the classroom when trying to design and implement self-directed learning. Once I collected their responses, I began the task of coding in order to identify themes and analyze the data to address a different "Now what?" question: that is, "I have all this information. Now what do I do with it?"

To help organize and code the responses of the participants, I used Quirkos, a qualitative analysis software program that allows users to drag and drop text from responses into colored "bubble" categories on the screen. The bubbles increase in size with the amount of coded material dropped into them. In that way, users clearly see the commonalities among the respondents, the trends, and the areas that could then move from initial coding to themes. When users click on any of the bubbles, they can see comments from all of the respondents that have been included, providing quick access for comparisons.

For my data collection, the bigger bubbles guided me directly to the best places to explore patterns, commonalities, and even contrasting views among the responses to see more clearly what exactly respondents have experienced with attempts to implement self-directed learning in their classes. Bigger bubbles, for example, such as "Scaffolding" and "Relational" and "Community," indicate the specific areas of challenges as well as successes that educators have experienced. Some of the comments in those respective bubbles are also cross-bubbled into the greater, general categories of "challenges" or "successes" or even specific programs such as "PLTW." All of these helped reveal themes and areas to begin focusing on in my next round of analysis.

Using the software to analyze thematic responses and cross-code them, I could see the common struggles and strategies that educators found useful for establishing support systems before implementing self-directed learning. Overall, this approach established a fairly clear route for exploring the guiding questions of the questionnaire through data analysis, as detailed in the sections below.

GUIDING QUESTION 1: HOW CAN WE DESIGN AND IMPLEMENT WAYS TO DEVELOP SELF-DIRECTED LEARNERS?

The first question—How can we design and implement effective ways to develop self-directed learners?—is the overarching essential question of the study and attempts to explore the end game of teaching. If, as contemporary research suggested, one primary purpose of education is to create self-directed learners, then the question of how to accomplish that is necessary to address before, and perhaps after, all others. The respondents of my questionnaire provided insightful information on this topic.

For many respondents, the foundation of this task lies less in curriculum and assessment than in intentional relationships, strategy, and support. Figure 4.1 illustrates this dynamic of how the broader question of effective design and implementation filters through these foundational concepts.

Figure 4.1 attempts to illustrate the questionnaire responses that indicate the foundational need to establish relationships, create strategies, and develop support, sometimes in ways that interconnect, before attempting to design and implement self-directed learning. Similar to the framework conceived of by Salina et al. (2016b) to build vibrant learning communities in general,

The Investment 49

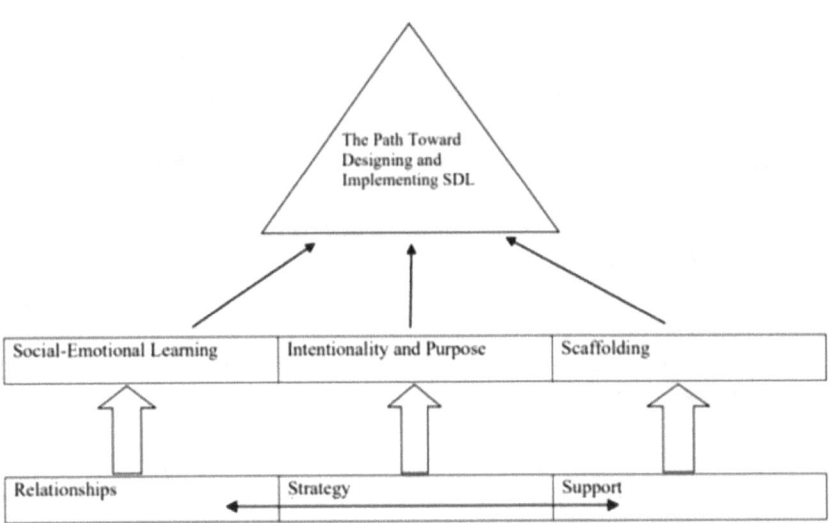

Figure 4.1. The Path toward Implementing Self-Directed Learning.

the multi-tiered framework that illustrates the responses to my questionnaire builds the capacity for self-directed learning to happen in their own learning communities. If we don't create intentional plans toward building relationships with students, implement strategies for purposeful learning and provide the much-needed support that functions as necessary scaffolding for that learning to occur, then our efforts will stall very quickly—whether those efforts aim toward self-directedness or anything else productive.

Among the responses that addressed the need to establish strong relationships with students, Principal Ryan Feehan said in his response that the "most critical aspect of the educational relationship is trust . . . built between a student and a teacher." Furthermore, Emily Torres said that relationships are at the core of her English classes, especially the "social-emotional focus." Karissa Jacobson also discussed the foundational need to build trust with students in her special education and co-taught English courses.

Darci Hastings spoke about how important relationships and community have been in her PLTW course, stating, "Creating community . . . has gotten to be a critical aspect of the course," while Tom Rye talked about building a "strong community" in his math classes. Spanish teacher Tamara Gower, meanwhile, discussed the need "to build . . . an inclusive, fun classroom community in which each student desires to engage in ways that feel comfortable." For Dr. Minaz Jooma, developing strong relationships is imperative toward helping students become more self-confident in their academic work—particularly self-directed academic work. All the respondents overwhelmingly pointed to the need to establish relationships and build community, and to address the social-emotional learning needs of students, before implementing the curriculum.

Respondents also addressed the overarching question of how to develop self-directed learners by discussing the need to go into this venture with a strategy, planning with intentionality and purpose. In many ways, their responses to this dovetailed with the priority of building relationships. As Karissa Jacobson said about her co-teaching experience, "As a team, we set up the self-directed learning experience" with a variety of relationship-building activities. Meanwhile, in Japanese classes, Shiho Ogata, or Ogata Sensei as she is known to her students, talked about balancing the goal for students to be creative, independent learners with the reality that many "current students need a great amount of guided learning to be successful."

Ogata Sensei's remarks indicated the concomitant need to build intentionally both in terms of curriculum and support. Ashley Jones also addressed the need to be intentional about both aspects in English class by commenting on the intentional scaffolding and planning that sets up self-directed experiences. Ryan Feehan spoke further about how intentional planning and guidance "reminds students that they are not on the journey alone and will receive as much support as they need to be successful."

The scaffolding, according to respondents, includes a variety of strategies. For instance, theology teacher Adam Galvez said he spends at least a quarter of the year intentionally modeling the strategies of self-directed learning before asking students to engage in that level of work. Galvez and Emily Torres both said that essential questions frequently set up student inquiry, as did James Noble, whose questions help "focus students," while Jim Wickes pointed to the importance of giving "initial guidance" before nudging students further into the realm of inquiry.

Enithie Hunter pointed to the Harkness Method as a structure at her school in New Jersey to help plan for purposeful, scaffolded independent learning. As she said in her response, scaffolding and modeling of the Harkness Method, which includes student-led discussions, peer review, and capstone projects, set up the actual self-directed learning experiences.

Similarly, Brad Koshka spoke about the "four pillars" that his school used to set up self-directedness with intentionality and support: namely, teacher advisors, personalized scheduling, customized learning, and authentic assessment. By planning strategically with these four guiding principles, Koshka addressed the strategies employed to establish a foundation for independent learning.

While the respondents addressed the foundations needed to start creating self-directed learning experiences, they also pointed to the very real challenges and obstacles in the way of the implementation of their designs.

GUIDING QUESTION 2: WHAT CHALLENGES AND OBSTACLES STAND IN THE WAY OF DESIGNING AND IMPLEMENTING SELF-DIRECTED LEARNING?

Even with intentional strategies to build trusting relationships with students, plan purposeful learning experiences, and provide necessary supports, respondents revealed tensions at the foundations of their work to develop self-directed learners. Some of the more predictable culprits of educational progress, such as time and restrictive curriculum, appeared as challenges and obstacles, as did others, such as the difficulties students had transitioning from traditional to more self-directed learning environments. Additional obstacles included deep-rooted systemic structures and engagement issues that respondents saw connected to the COVID-19 pandemic.

When thinking specifically about designing and implementing self-directed learning experiences, many of the respondents identified one of the first and most obvious challenges as time and the amount of time it takes to make self-directed learning happen in their classes. Ashley Jones, Emily Torres, and Tom Rye all pointed directly to challenges of time, with Rye acknowledging, on the one hand, the value of the approach to inquiry but, on the other hand, conceding it was difficult to find the time "to create a worthwhile experience."

Furthermore, educators pointed to layers of time challenges, such as time management, both on the part of teachers and students. As Sensei pointed out in her response, the task of monitoring individual work in the context of simultaneous large-group settings presented challenges. Trying to manage "the big class as I am giving more choices and creating . . . materials to meet their needs/interests within limited time" became prohibitive as did the need to "connect with individual students . . . and give them appropriate feedback" on their work. Ultimately, she said that she "needed more time" to accomplish this type of work as effectively as she would prefer.

Adam Galvez addressed another issue of time management: namely, the students and their varying abilities to manage their own time during self-directed tasks. "With all the freedom offered by self-directed learning," he said, "it can be difficult to track student progress in a meaningful way." Tamara Gower added that it is problematic when "I provide the gift of work time in class, but some students do not know how (or choose not) to" capitalize on that work time. Brad Koshka discussed interventions related to time management that his school took while guiding students such as checkpoints called "Task Verification" to meet with students periodically and make sure that they were on track with their self-directed projects. Ryan Feehan expanded on these structured check-ins by saying that they led to "soft boundaries and timelines" to keep students on pace.

Karissa Jacobson spoke specifically to the problem of the time required to plan for differentiated instruction in a tenth-grade co-taught English class in which student abilities ranged from second-grade reading levels to students with extremely advanced skills.

These challenges were connected, according to the responses, to planning time and the need to have consistent, productive collaboration to design these experiences. As Koshka said, "This approach does not work if teachers insist on working in isolation." For that challenge to be met, a "Collaborative Response Model" was needed to ensure that planning time happened.

Along with time and time management, respondents identified restrictive curriculum demands as problematic. Jim Wickes, for instance, admitted to not designing self-directed learning experiences for students in large part because of an established, structured curriculum already in place. With "clear learning goals . . . from either state standards or the overarching frameworks of the AP Lit course," in place, Wickes did not feel the freedom to explore self-directed learning in his classes.

It's important to note that Jim's experiences reflect many teachers across the country: excellent, accomplished, veteran teachers who do purposeful work in the class but, for one reason or another, do not feel the freedom (or, in some cases—but not necessarily Jim's case—the need) to implement self-directed learning. I have all the respect in the world for Jim and value the work he does with his students.

Similarly, Tom Rye pointed to the obstacle of restrictive curriculum in math. "Each of my classes," wrote Rye, "has a clearly defined curriculum designated by external sources. This gives a fixed nature to the learning goals" and makes it difficult for students to engage directly in self-directed learning. At the same time, Rye said that "the spirit of self-directed learning may be incorporated" into his classes with big ideas such as "reasoning, problem-solving, and communication." While Rye talked about his classes being student-centered places of inquiry and collaboration, he did acknowledge the distinction between the concept of self-directed learning as defined by Knowles and the nuanced circumstances of most math classes, especially regarding the role of students selecting their own learning goals.

Tom's points regarding math instruction are important to note and align with the research others have done on the topic (Khan et al., 2012; Sumantri and Satriani, 2016; Liljedahl, 2021). While approaches to self-directed learning can happen and offer benefits to math students, these must honor the nuances of the discipline. In other words, the way an English teacher attempts to implement self-directed learning and the degree of guidance one teacher might need to offer will depend on the subject. As Mehta and Fine (2019) found in their comprehensive study of schools around the United States, even schools that aim to be project-based and inquiry-driven "struggle when it comes to integrating math into their model" (p. 85). As Tom said, the spirit of inquiry can still drive instruction, but it will reflect the principles of mathematics and the idea that, as Mehta and Fine discovered, it's "less about knowing the right answers" and more about exploration, collaboration, and revision (p. 324). As one teacher in their study said, math is about "empowering students" (p. 324).

The work of Boaler (2002) and Meyer (2023) has given math teachers ample ideas and strategies for empowering students and fostering their spirit of inquiry. Liljedahl (2021), meanwhile, has delineated multiple classroom strategies for helping students to become strong, people of inquiry through mathematics by presenting specific issues in the math classroom, considering problems related to those issues, and then exploring strategies that move students toward thinking critically and mathematically. The challenges for math instruction are real but not insurmountable toward developing self-directedness.

Darci Hastings, meanwhile, spoke of the disjuncture between science classes with fixed standards and her highly individualized and self-directed Biomedical Innovations research course, a culminating class in the PLTW series at Ferris. When students are not used to working in a self-directed way due to the restrictive nature of other curricula, then they find the transition to her course quite challenging at times. "Some students," she wrote, "find it really difficult to think outside the box—their entire scientific career in school has been a teacher presenting them with information, lab protocols that are supposed to work 'just right,' etc." When they participate in her course, she explained, they must "learn how to be independent thinkers and learners."

Because so much of the school system is based on set curriculum and standards, respondents commented that students frequently struggled when placed in open-ended, self-directed learning environments. As James Noble said of students in his social studies courses, they "struggled with the open nature of the work and often became frustrated with the length of the process" and the "lack of 'concrete answers.'" This made it difficult for them, he said, to work on projects that seemed too complex, led to procrastination or shutting down completely, and struggling or failing to accomplish the tasks in "a reasonable amount of time," pointing back to the issues of time involved in this process as well as the struggles students had moving from traditional to more self-directed learning.

Enithie Hunter commented on this dynamic as well, recalling her experiences in her previous school, a public school in the Atlanta area, where her experiments with self-directed learning were met with resistance not only from students but also colleagues and administrators. Students, she said, were "unaccustomed to both the level of autonomy and accountability required," while colleagues worried the approach might lead to "a standard they were not prepared or comfortable with," and administrators who were "uncomfortable with how it might impact standardized test scores."

These obstacles and challenges lead to other problematic factors, such as the tension between providing engaging, independent learning experiences and lowering the standards or defaulting to what Freire called the "banking" approach to education—teachers providing direct input to passive student receivers of that information. As Ashley Jones said, it becomes "easier to design lessons where students take a passive role and are receiving information rather than constructing it." Galvez's responses concurred, as he discussed the danger of "allowing students to choose their own adventure can lead to low-stakes inquiry" and can lead to "dragging" the baseline which in turn leads to "headaches for teachers."

Some of these problems were exacerbated by the COVID-19 pandemic, as many of the respondents noted. Galvez, for example, discussed the tension between "the frequency of self-paced assessments" during the online learning that took place during COVID quarantines and the "lowering of standards" that made school "even more difficult and less rewarding." James Noble discussed the challenges of helping students when they were online. Students, said Noble, "many times gave up when they were unsure how to proceed." This problem followed students when they returned to campus learning: "They seemed to lack the resiliency to move beyond the 'text' and become comfortable with uncertainty." Furthermore, the transition from online learning back to a more traditionally structured on-campus learning environment became "an obstacle to some students, while the many absences due to being sick, caring for sick family members, and apathy of being in school present major obstacles."

Ogata Sensei, meanwhile, found it difficult to maintain some of the student-directed activities she used in classes before the pandemic. Her highly personalized learning center activities, for example, in which students could choose from multiple activities to explore aspects of language learning, became difficult to monitor during COVID. She did modify it, though, to simplify the approach and encourage routes for cultural exploration. She planned to continue that model after the pandemic.

Enithie Hunter commented, moreover, that some of the challenges she saw during the pandemic actually started beforehand. When she began teaching at her school which uses the Harkness Method to foster self-directed learning, she noticed a higher level of student engagement and self-regulation than exists today. "Recently (and it's important to note that this *began* before COVID), I've noticed that students are less likely to be prepared, less likely to listen carefully to others . . . and less likely to self-regulate without adult intervention."

For Dr. Jooma, the developing needs of students beyond merely the scholastic has heightened her intentions to identify the learning needs of her students as well as their individual "aptitudes, proclivities, and anxieties" and address them in "more nuanced, varied, practical, and healthy ways."

The responses addressing challenges and obstacles came from a variety of disciplines, regions, and perspectives. All pointed to specific ways that creating and implementing self-directed learning can include problems that the respondents felt needed individualized and collaborative efforts to solve.

GUIDING QUESTION 3: WHAT WILL WE LEARN ABOUT OURSELVES AND OUR SCHOOL CULTURE AS WE EXPLORE WAYS TO DEVELOP SELF-DIRECTED LEARNERS?

Many of the respondents reflected on their practice, overall, as educators when working through the questionnaire. Ashley Jones, for example, wondered how much she actually incorporated true self-directed learning in her classes. As she said, "I often have to stop and remind myself of my learning goals for the students" and not worry so much about content coverage, which she called "the greatest adversary to self-directed learning." James Noble, similarly, reflected on his perceived shortcomings. "I am not as creative an educator," he said, "as I'd like to be" and said he struggled with "the 'messiness' of having students moving in different directions." Tamara Gower also commented on the struggle to balance the messiness of a self-directed approach to learning with the obstacles and challenges noted above. She concluded, however, that the challenge is worth the struggle. "Bring on the mess," she wrote. "If we do not teach students how to attend to their individual selves and urge them to use and trust their instincts to learn new things," then, she wrote, "I am concerned about the future. But I do believe that with good modeling and coaching, young learners will continue to change the tides toward self-directed learning to better themselves and inspire their communities." She is realistic about the struggle yet optimistic about the possibilities.

Along with that belief in the struggle came many reflections and examples of successes with the approach. For example, Jones, despite her self-doubts, commented on the successes she has had with self-directed opportunities for her students. "For me," she said, "self-directed learning has led to more inquiry" and has made her "more intentional" as a designer of learning experiences. Noble reflected on the success of his AP Seminar students, who enrolled in the elective course, "were highly motivated," and thrived in college due to the course and its ability to prepare them for higher education.

Karissa Jacobson, meanwhile, reflected on the successes her students had with self-directed learning, both in co-taught English and in her resource class. She talked about how many students "want to be challenged and given choices," to have opportunities to "show off what they excel at," and to showcase their talents in ways that do more than simply build individual skills. In fact, she wrote, self-directed learning experiences "build community and relationships."

When this happens, Jacobson wrote, students grow in confidence by exploring ideas in their own ways and presenting their learning "in a format that fits their learning style best" and fulfilling some of the goals for the course, which Jacobson said was to see students as the drivers "in their learning journey. They might take a road we would never imagine," she added, "which is not only exciting for the student but for us as well!" She did acknowledge the constant need to continue to explore further ways for her resource students to experience that more frequently.

For Emily Torres, inquiry-driven, project-based learning frequently served as a vehicle for self-directedness. Starting with essential questions and building on prior knowledge and skills, students must explore and create personalized projects that they present to others in the community at large. Doing so, wrote Torres, created community connections that are "key so [students] can see the importance of learning outside the classroom walls." As a result, some of her students have published original poetry, won prizes in essay competitions, and have even been invited to the Washington State Capitol to accept awards for their work.

Likewise, Darci Hasting's students have experienced a great deal of success through her research class. As she wrote, her program is the only one in eastern Washington "to qualify a student to the International Science and Engineering Fair (ISEF) for six straight years." Her students have won awards, scholarships, and prizes that have led to international distinctions and success in higher education—both at the undergraduate level and in graduate and medical schools. Hastings reported that many of her students, now in grad school, tell her that "the skills they learned in research class helped them" in post-graduate work.

Hastings noted, too, that the success was not limited to students who would traditionally be considered top of the class. She noted the "students that struggle academically for many reasons and are still able to design, carry out, and present a project" stand out to her as definite success stories.

In that same spirit, the course in environmental chemistry that Hastings and her teaching partner, Diane Cortner, designed aims to lead students who have struggled academically toward successful experiences in the discipline. By structuring the course as self-paced, teachers turn over much control of the learning to students to work on a schedule and in ways that match their readiness. Differentiated learning options and labs allow students to choose their paths, giving the teachers more time to work as guides and support for those students along the way. While students in this class are not gearing their work toward international science competitions the way Hastings' PLTW students are, they are nonetheless learning the art and science of inquiry in a way that grows more naturally out of their interests and readiness. Success comes in different forms.

IMPLICATIONS

The respondents to my questionnaire provided candid, insightful (and inspiring!) answers—as well as further questions—about their experiences while trying to design and implement self-directed learning in their classes. Specifically, they offered insights into the three guiding questions:

1) How can we design and implement ways to develop self-directed learners?
2) What challenges and obstacles stand in the way of designing and implementing self-directed learning?
3) What will we learn about ourselves and our school culture as we explore ways to develop self-directed learners?

By listening to the responses of my colleagues and analyzing their experiences, I have been able to organize and articulate the varied challenges, obstacles, and successes they have encountered on a regular basis. This analysis transcends informal chatting during passing periods between classes and helps to set up reflective, intentional planning based on qualitative data.

Some of their experiences include the ever-present challenges of time management, intentional planning, and supportive structures that allow for intentional planning. Furthermore, a priority on building relationships with students, designing ways to support them, and helping them transition from pandemic protocols to post-pandemic routines and expectations are all crucial realities for educators. While the protocols may have shifted back to those we practiced before the pandemic, much of the trauma from the pandemic remains for many and must be considered when working with students. Finally, a frequent disjuncture between the established standards and authentic learning exists in many classes and needs attention, querying, and rethinking in order to guide students toward more self-directed experiences.

The constant challenges of time and time management range from curricular restrictions in some cases to issues of intrinsic motivation in others. While acknowledging the curricular restrictions that exist in some disciplines, schools, districts, and even states, I would also say that, based on the responses to my questionnaire, it is imperative within those restrictions for educators to find ways to rethink their use of time in order to maximize students engagement in the long run. This is not an easy task and certainly takes courage, trial, and error; in the end, however, the stakes are too high to surrender too readily to time constraints.

As Ashley Jones pointed out in the questionnaire, she often has to remind herself of her purpose and goals in order to avoid mere coverage, which can kill the true spirit of inquiry and authentic learning. Instead of defaulting to a banking method of school for the sake of time or, as Adam Galvez pointed out, permitting "low-stakes inquiry" to happen because it is easier, faster, and more expedient, teachers need to pause periodically and, as much as possible, consider how they want to budget the allotted time they have with their students each day.

Using essential questions to spark interest, for instance, can be a useful strategy to lead students into problem-posing, as long as teachers are willing to let the exploration of those questions drift into areas that were not part of the initial plan or vision of the educator while designing the lesson. It can be scary to live in the "messiness" of true inquiry, as James Noble put it, but it can also develop into an atmosphere of joy and insight when students are allowed to run with their ideas. I have seen this happen in Noble's classes many times over the years that I have worked with him, and his students thrive because of his encouragement and nurturing.

If, however, essential questions are simply posted on a classroom wall or are not allowed to foster true inquiry, then they become another wasted opportunity and irrelevant wall decoration along with the other signs intended for education yet ignored in practice.

To make inquiry happen, teachers need to set aside time for authentic collaboration in which they investigate strategies together, ask each other what works and what does not work, and experiment with their ideas in the class. Administration can play a significant role in this process. As Brad Koshka pointed out, his school used several "pillars" to guide their implementation process—including a "collaborative response model" that allowed teachers to partake in that crucial work of curricular design and implementation.

Without the support and overall buy-in of administration, teachers can often feel like their efforts are almost dead before they start, as Enithie Hunter experienced in one of her former learning communities in which colleagues and administrators were not comfortable with the self-directed approach Hunter wanted to take with her students. Fortunately, she found a more supportive community later with support and intentional structures in place like the Harkness Method to nurture self-directed learning.

It is important to remember, too, that before hoping to engage students in this type of learning, their social-emotional needs must be addressed sufficiently. As teacher after teacher in the questionnaire responded, students must feel like they are in a place of safety and community. They must trust teachers to be led down a road of inquiry. For this reason, too, the data for this capstone points toward a need to re-envision how classroom time is used. The seemingly robust notion of teaching "bell-to-bell" appeals to some who conjure Dickens' Mr. Gradgrind and insist on stringent education methods. An arguably more effective approach, however, and one that more accurately reflects the data, involves developing the inquiry process in students through a level of trust and understanding that teachers are on the side of students and, again, functioning as Freirean partners in problem-posing.

The time it takes, therefore, to build community must be intentional, as Karissa Jacobson pointed out, and the implementation of it must be authentic and valued. It cannot be seen as artificial, mechanical processes in an isolated part of class; rather, social-emotional learning and relationship building must be at the core of the class. For instance, time dedicated to community building during the first five minutes of a period can and must be carried through the academic lesson and work before it takes root in learners who want to see more than anything that the adults in their lives care about them and are willing to invest in them—not just academically but also emotionally—to the point of sacrificing bell-to-bell instructional time. Ultimately, do we want students to remember the difference between independent and dependent clauses, or do we want them to remember that they had adults in their corner pulling for them and working to help them succeed? Based on the responses to the questionnaires, the answer is clear.

That said, emotional support only goes so far in the classroom, and students still need to be challenged academically and guided into and through the inquiry process. This takes tremendous skill and understanding of when to push, when to pause, and when to hold back or redirect the learning momentum. As Adam Galvez pointed out in his questionnaire response, he invests significant class time in modeling the learning and inquiry habits he wants students to develop. Darci Hastings must teach her PLTW students how to be learners before sending them into their own pursuits. In other words, self-directed learning does not simply happen on its own. Teachers must work hard to design, implement, and reflect on this work to see what, in fact, works and what needs to be reconsidered. With that in mind, the reality of collaboration—as mentioned above—is even more critical to teachers if they want to move toward this approach with any hope of seeing it take root in their students.

Their students, after all, may find themselves being transitioned into post-pandemic protocols; however, many of them have yet to move emotionally or physically away from the actual trauma experienced during the pandemic. The aftermath is significant for everyone, and the planning, support, and implementation must be managed carefully and purposefully each step of the way. The work of Salina et al. (2016b) around relationships, academic press, and social-emotional needs seems more relevant than ever in the post-pandemic context and could be a valuable resource for learning communities as they begin to work strategically toward these aims with their students.

By planning intentionally and strategically with scaffolding in place to guide and support students along the way while using existing frameworks and planning tools such as backward design and differentiated instruction, educators give themselves a better chance of creating and implementing experiences that help their students become more independent, self-efficacious, and self-directed learners.

SUMMARY

Candid responses from educators concerning the obstacles, challenges, and successes they have faced while trying to design and implement self-directed learning provided insights into the realities of teaching in secondary schools in a post-pandemic context. Qualitative analysis software helped identify common threads and connections among the responses that pointed to three main areas that should be prioritized by schools before attempting to implement self-directed learning: namely, relationship building that addresses social-emotional needs in authentic ways; intentional strategies to create purposeful learning experiences for all students; and, last but not least, methodical support that creates the scaffolding needed to make that purposeful learning happen. Without those three foundational elements, the conditions are not ready for self-directed learning.

Chapter 5

Now What?

Besides being an incredible math teacher, Tom Rye is also a nationally recognized professional developer. In this role, he has delivered timely, relevant training in instructional design to schools and districts across the country. One of his consistent reminders to workshop participants has been this gem: "Professional development is not revolutionary but evolutionary." I love that. Our growth as educators rarely leaps from novice to expert overnight; our insights rarely come out of thin air. More frequently, our insights build from experiences gradually and connectively. Instead of developing professionally in a clean, linear manner, our growth tends to be messy and recursive. We must therefore draw on our past experiences and previous learning, building on them to enhance and advance our work with students.

The candid reflections and insights offered by my colleagues in the previous chapter provide a realistic portrait of such experiences and learning. They especially depict the challenges and recursive processes teachers face when trying to implement self-directed learning. The responses of these educators, when paired with contemporary research, provide important data to help strategize ideas and solutions for our own classes. When, for example, we prioritize relationships as emphatically as the respondents did in the questionnaire, along with academic rigor and intentional structure, we can then build from those foundational concepts purposefully and give students the proper environment to begin exploring self-directed learning in productive, sustainable ways.

Educators, then, face the challenge of addressing all three of these foundational elements pertaining to their learning communities given the contextualized and nuanced needs of their students, as well as the deeply rooted biases and routines of their own practices. They must take what they already do well and add the insights of other educators and researchers. In this chapter,

I would like to offer routes—not prescriptions or rigid programs—to accomplish that goal in order to create contextualized, practical ways to develop self-directed learning experiences for students. From there, I will consider the implications of this work and why it is so urgent in today's secondary schools.

AUTHENTIC RELATIONSHIPS, ACADEMIC STRATEGY, AND STRUCTURAL SUPPORT

Addressing all three of these crucial aspects of learning—authentic relationships, academic strategy, and structural support—can be a daunting task, specifically within the context of self-directed learning. However, if each one is considered as a part of the whole and looked at one at a time, then the task becomes rather more manageable—especially when keeping in mind that most educators do at least some of these things already in their work.

Authentic Relationships

While several specific programs on the market can help to foster and facilitate relationship-building in the classroom, sometimes the most effective work comes down to committing to invest in the lives of students by listening to them and demonstrating care for them. According to DeBarger (2021), "Care is foundational to agency" because it validates students, creates trust, and leads to confident risk-taking. When I think of the work Emily Torres does with her students, I think of an example of how teachers can build those caring relationships authentically and strategically without running an expensive, pre-packaged program.

When Emily started to recognize the growing need to address the social-emotional needs of students caused specifically by trauma, she took steps to address those needs in order to help the mental health of her students which could then pave the way for their academic work. While she teaches Honors classes and has taught nearly every level of secondary English, she has a specific passion for trauma-based learning. Acting on that passion, she has taken intentional steps to develop expertise in the area, including the completion of a training course through the Community Resilience Initiative, through which she has also served as a presenter in holistic classrooms. Additionally, she has provided trauma-based and holistic-classroom professional development for her school district.

For Emily, the classroom is a community for the whole child. While academics are crucial, academic needs and student potential cannot be met until the emotional needs of students are addressed as well. To that end,

Emily sets up the physical space of her classroom to include ambient lighting, alternate seating arrangements, and fidget devices such as exercise balls and even exercise bikes. She spends consistent time with gratitude journals and other techniques to help students focus, deal with their emotional needs, and prepare to learn in a safe, nurturing space. Once a week, she brings in a psychologist who works with her students as well. For her, authentic relationships are developed by addressing the social-emotional needs of her students in strategic ways.

Ultimately, she brings this work full circle by tying it directly back to the academic learning she does with her students. For example, while teaching classics such as *The Crucible* or *The Great Gatsby*, Emily facilitates learning activities that make intentional connections between the text and the concepts addressed by the psychologist. As a result, students feel safe, supported, and valued in her classes—and much more authentically connected with the texts they study. Because they know she cares deeply about them as people, they feel safe to take academic risks that they might not be willing to take otherwise. The time Emily loses from explicit academic instruction to do this holistic learning is more than gained back by the return she gets from her students.

While this particular work is not self-directed, it addresses the foundational need for students to feel valued in an authentic way and engage in self-directed learning. In other words, the experiences Emily designs for her students set up the conditions for self-directedness to succeed. It is one of the three foundational steps that lead to self-directedness, and Emily does it as well as anyone.

That is not to say, of course, Emily's is the only way to do it. Teachers have for years developed strategies to meet the social-emotional needs of students. A specific program is not as important as a consistent tone and expression of kindness, an intentional caring for students who are real people with real, complex needs. To go back to Mehta and Fine, it's about adults who care deeply about their students and take the time to show them that they care.

At this point, readers might take stock of their own classes and ask to what extent they design intentional strategies to implement relationship-building. Figure 5.1 offers a space for reflection and brainstorming on this topic.

For me, a shift in this regard began evolving over the years as I took stock of the social-emotional needs of my students. While I always felt like I did a pretty good job establishing rapport with students and creating an enjoyable learning environment, I also saw the benefits of building clear, consistent time in class to develop those relational, community skills that would lead to better learning in the long run. As I looked for ways to be more intentional about this aspect of teaching, I found myself drawn to other learning

What are three specific strategies I currently use to establish authentic relationships with my students?

1. _____
2. _____
3. _____

In my experience, how have authentic relationships with students correlated with academic engagement and success?

What could I do differently to build relationships with students as authentically as possible to prepare them for self-directed learning?

Figure 5.1. Establishing Authentic Relationships.

communities that seemed to do school completely differently from the typical American setup.

In Finland, for example, consistent space is set aside during the school day for breaks between lessons (Hancock, 2011; Jackson, 2016). While this might pertain specifically to younger students in the article, I found that my high schoolers needed that time as well. Accordingly, I decided to move beyond the traditional anticipatory set of a typical lesson plan and craft strategic brain breaks that showed the same value of play as the Finnish model, provided brain breaks, and built authentic relationships. Each day would feature a different community-building activity: myRead Monday, Team-Challenge Tuesday, Writing on Wednesday, Throwback Thursday, and Fun-Fact Friday.

The time devoted to choice reading, brainteasers, creative writing, trivia challenges, and games has become a critical part of my classes. Both my co-taught classes and my AP classes benefit from these structured times of seemingly unstructured, unacademic activity. There tends to be a sense of letting down one's hair, forgetting about the stress of the day, and laughing a lot. In many ways, the aim of this time aligns with the idea of *ubuntu*, discussed earlier, in that it connects students to their learning community as valued members who grow out of that community, are supported by others in it, and ultimately contribute to it. We spend this time together because we value each other as people and as learners working together to develop our individual qualities.

Again, the time I lose from direct academic instruction—anywhere between five-to-ten minutes on average—seems more than made up for by the relationships I build with my students and that they build with each other. In the co-taught classes, this sense of play is particularly essential as students see two adults being goofy and showing genuine care for them. As that play builds community and relationships, students tend to settle in more readily and seem more emotionally prepared to do the academic work at hand.

Exceptions to this exist, of course, and not all students respond to the approach. In such cases, my co-teacher Karissa Jacobson and I need to seek other strategies with the students (and sometimes the parent, counselor, or other support staff) to help them feel valued and emotionally prepared to work. It's a real challenge. On the one hand, it seems like play (because it *is* play); on the other hand, it is play intentionally designed to help move students toward feeling valued, more confident, and more prepared to take academic risks. The stakes are high. Overall, students have responded to this approach positively.

And what about grades and test scores? Has the time given over to play hurt the academic progress in class? While I feel confident that my pass rates and exam scores would support my teaching strategies (e.g., 96 percent of my students scored at least a 3 on their AP exam in 2022 and 2023), I would again take my cues from the teachers in Finland who not only value play but also view tests and scores with a healthy skepticism. As principal Timo Heikkinen said, "If you only measure the statistics, you miss the human aspect" (p. 4). Furthermore, these educators seem to value thinking and process more than work rate and product. "We prepare children how to learn," said Pasi Sahlberg, a math and physics teacher who eventually worked for Finland's Ministry of Education and Culture, "not how to take a test" (p. 6).

For me, grading is an ongoing challenge to help students see an accurate representation of the work they have done in my class. While the topic of grading merits a separate study, I will say that over the years I've tried multiple approaches and currently find myself returning to the idea of contract grading that focuses more on the process of work and offering students feedback than on points or traditional grading methods (Tchudi, 1996; Zerwin, 2020; Czarnecki, 2023). Overall, contract or labor-based grading seems more aligned with the ideals of self-directedness. If I want to put students in the driver's seat of their own learning, why would I continue to withhold the keys to the car? That's what traditional grading feels like much of the time. Again, though, that's a topic for another day.

Back to Finland. While I am not naïve enough to think the schools in Finland are perfect or devoid of challenges, I do think their points of emphasis have paid off, overall, to indicate they are on to something important and worth emulating. Given the country's top performances in the Programme for International Student Assessment in which they outranked the test-heavy schools in the United States, I will take my chances with relationship-building and alternatives to grading.

Whatever team-building, community-building, or relationship-building approach you prefer, just use *something* positive to establish with students that you care about them not just for what they can do for your school's test scores. Let them know that that is not why you are there. You are there because you care about them as people and are willing to do whatever it takes to support them, elevate their humanity (even if it means lowering your own dignity through goofy games in class), and help them become the best version of themselves. The message might not come through initially for some, especially those who bring scars into class from numerous previous experiences with adults who have decidedly not cared about them. Your consistent messaging, however, while never perfectly delivered, will pay off in the end.

Academic Strategy

We build relationships not as a gimmick or a trick to "get kids to learn." We build relationships because that is a critical part of what we do as teachers: we value people and want them to understand how important they are to us and their community. At the same time, we also want them to push themselves and achieve things academically that they didn't think they could achieve before they entered our class. We want them to understand that learning is important and that they are worth the investment to become better learners. We understand from the research and from experience that strong relationships build trust and the capacity for students to take safe risks in their own learning.

As Dr. Minaz Jooma said in her questionnaire response, developing relationships that strengthen the self-confidence of students is foundational to preparing them for the academic challenges she guides them through during her classes. When she works individually with students to provide honest feedback during conferences, she aims to do so in a way that also builds self-efficacy. Students who respond to her honest yet supportive feedback tend to progress as writers and grow in confidence. For Dr. Jooma, this growth is vital to the educational experience: "we built up his confidence and equipped him to manage his learning as he applied self-directed learning methods to attain greater proficiency in ELA skills and increased his reading skills in particular." She invests in students not simply to help them succeed academically but, more importantly, because she cares deeply about them and wants them to see how much they can achieve as strong, capable people.

With that in mind, we owe it to our students to create strategic, purposeful learning experiences for those students we care about so much; not to do so would be short-changing them and also falling short of our professional calling. Accordingly, if we are going to set up self-directed learning experiences, then we must work with particular intentionality to create those academic conditions and challenges for students.

While I already traced a couple of ways to create learning experiences based on established frameworks such as *Understanding by Design* and *Differentiated Instruction*, I absolutely know that numerous strategies exist to move students into the driver's seat of their learning and nurture self-directedness. Darci Hastings reflected in chapter 4 about the role Project Lead the Way has played in helping her science students develop their self-directedness; Enithie Hunter spoke about the Harkness Method in a similar way. When teachers can draw on established frameworks and work within the guiding principles of programs, they can leverage those resources readily to help students become deeper thinkers. What, however, are some specific strategies that help students develop their skills as self-directed learners?

Ogata Sensei, Tamara Gower, and the World Language Department at Ferris have used choice activities and self-paced learning centers to move students toward self-directedness. While the pandemic made those activities especially difficult to monitor, they have tried to re-introduce them strategically into their classes. In these contexts, students explore specific language skills, targets, and cultural aspects of the language that they can learn either individually or in small groups. Each activity occupies its own physical space in the classroom, and students literally move around the room to try out the activities. The activity can resemble the stations of an elementary or even a Montessori class with adjustments appropriate to secondary learning, including the accounting for developmental and cognitive maturation.

Sensei has found that re-integrating those activities requires re-training students to be independent and effective managers of their own time; many of her students need that re-training. Rather than doing large, free-choice projects four times a year, as she did pre-pandemic, she only does them twice a year in order to make the work more manageable for her students and herself. The challenges she faces with her post-pandemic students are real, and the brainstorming that she, Gower, and others—presumably those reading this book—have done to rebuild those skills is both daunting and highly admirable. Their work is consistently difficult, and yet they have refused to quit on their students.

A couple of planning templates can help educators brainstorm and map out ways to move students into the driver's seat and empower them to engage in inquiry-based learning. The first template (figure 5.2) focuses on strategies to offer students choice in their learning and even assessment.

Unit Title:		
Big Ideas / Essential Questions / Goals / Standards / Learning Targets:		
Learning Option 1	Learning Option 2	Learning Option 3
Possible Accommodations		
Additional Planning Notes		

Figure 5.2. Template to Design Self-Directed Learning.

An outgrowth of the backward design template that Wiggins and McTighe developed (1998) aims to provide teachers with ways to design and implement intentional choices to students in the learning process. Significantly, it includes a section on accommodations for students in class with individualized learning plans. Simple by intent, it serves as a brainstorming map more than anything else and might prove especially useful to teachers beginning the journey of introducing choice that leads ultimately to self-directedness.

The second template (figure 5.3) provides design options, too, but does so in a rather more focused and in-depth way for teachers who are more confident in establishing routes for student self-directed learning. This template asks designers to consider several specific questions about purpose, standards, essential questions, choices, and the teacher role in the process.

After considering one of the above templates for brainstorming and design drafting, readers might want to pause yet again to reflect on some of the changes they have observed in their own practices, particularly with strategies for reaching students and engaging them in academic work, due to the pandemic and its lingering effects. Figure 5.4 provides space to reflect on those challenges and brainstorm solutions to rebuild or re-route student

Now What? 69

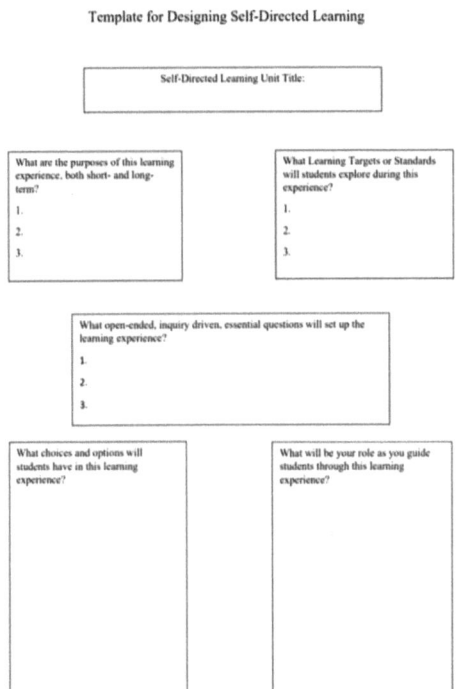

Figure 5.3. Engaging Students in Post-Pandemic Academic Work.

engagement in a post-pandemic context. Doing so will inform the design process, especially in terms of revision and clarifying next steps.

For instance, I have used the design templates in figures 5.2 and 5.3 and ones similar to them in my own teaching for years. After the pandemic, however, I realized that several key conditions had changed in my experience. Spending some reflective time helped clarify how to revise my usual plans and build more intentionally in the new context. Upon returning from online learning to resuming campus work, I noticed—as did many teachers—that more students were not just into their phones but were also seemingly dependent on them as if they were teddy bears to toddlers. After spending nearly a year using phones as their lifelines toward social connectivity, some students lacked the capacity to pry their eyes away from the world of safety offered in those tiny screens in their hands. What strategies have I had to implement and try . . . and fail at trying . . . and try again to help students re-enter non-screen life? How could the design templates help in that process?

Could I use the problem of phone addiction as a strength instead of simply a problem and point of frustration? I confess that I have not solved the

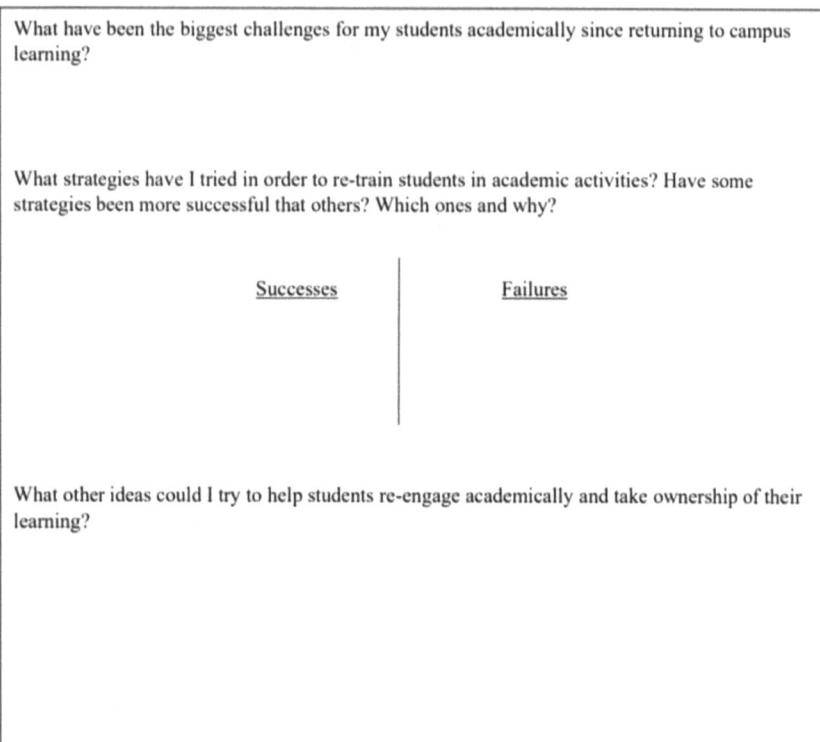

Figure 5.4. Challenges.

problem for all students; I have, however, found some success in incorporating phones into research, composition, and reading in ways that, I hope, could teach students to be productive, healthy users of media instead of falling into a black hole of screen scrolling. Furthermore, the work of Jenson and Droumeva (2017) in the area of technology use and gamification in the class has inspired me to explore innovative ways to set up my students for success. Again, though, I understand the constant challenge. The template in figure 5.4 does not pretend to produce easy answers to the problems of phones or other post-pandemic conditions. At the same time, by acknowledging the challenges and listing the successes as well as the failures, I feel a little more prepared to plan my next steps to help students find routes to being self-directed. I encourage readers to play around with the template in that spirit as well.

Take as much time and extra space as you need to reflect on these points. Perhaps something you did before the pandemic that always worked has stopped working since returning to "normal" conditions. How have you dealt with that new reality? For me, it has been like returning to a favorite fishing hole only to realize that many fish simply won't take the same bait they always used to take. I have had to rethink some very basic classroom practices as well as larger academic assignments in order to get students to re-engage authentically. My responses to this reality have been a mixture of frustration, excitement, dread, and hope all at the same time.

One of the academic revisions I have made has to do with the research-based literary analysis I typically assign seniors at the end of semester one. For years, I assigned the traditional research essay—a certain number of secondary resources, MLA format, well-crafted analysis, and so on. Once I started to figure out the value, however, of differentiation, I began offering choices to students that involved creative ways to blend their budding scholarship with their own strengths and interests. Over the past few years, and especially after the pandemic, I have rethought the project altogether. The advent of ChatGPT has further forced me to reconsider what, how, and why I would assign to students for them to demonstrate their analytical skills.

As a result of these developments and considerations, I modified the assignment to look like the one in figure 5.5.

This is quite the shift from the research assignments I gave years ago in which I instructed students to accomplish specific tasks of literary research based on limited prompts, texts, and resources. While I still established some parameters in this new assessment, I wanted to see how students could think outside of those traditional boundaries to create projects that reflected their own interests, personalities, connections, and pursuits. As the teacher, I am the guide. As Knowles said of his students in 1975, "They want teachers who know what they are doing . . . I have learned to emphasize that we shall be working within a structure" (p. 37). This is not a free for all in which I just turn them loose to do whatever they want. As a teacher, I have a role to play in partnering with students and guiding them (Freire, 1970; Tan, 2018).

That makes the process fun, however, as well as challenging for both me and my students. As I watch, guide, and redirect (to help cultivate their abilities to self-direct), I need to be aware of many deep-rooted practices and anxieties at work within many of their adolescent brains—some of which are far more developed than mine was at seventeen and some which are right on par with where mine was—and learn to listen to them to know how to guide them. Sometimes that includes direct coaching: "You haven't been doing anything for thirty minutes. It's time to get some work done." Sometimes that means hearing students who don't want to be self-directed: "Just tell us what to do, Mr. Powell!" And sometimes—many times—that involves simply listening to a student as they are in the middle of working through ideas and offering them assurance: "This looks great. Keep it up." The needs of students shift during the process, and my job is to know how to support their process (Dixon, 2016).

Extended Literary Analysis

AP English Literature and Composition

First Semester

Due: Friday, January 20th, 2023

This project will give you the opportunity to apply the skills you have developed this semester regarding literary analysis and composition. You will be able to explore the questions we've posed, the texts we've read, and the concepts we've considered in ways that I hope are fun and purposeful for you.

While I will need to see certain skills demonstrated, I also want to leave a lot of room for this to be an individualized, self-directed project in which you prioritize the learning goals and make choices from the texts that help you demonstrate your understanding of the course's big ideas.

To that end, here is the plan:

1. Choose one of the big questions we have explored this semester that interests you. Some of those questions include the following:
    a. How do we analyze literature, and why is it important?
    b. What makes a work of literature "great"?
    c. How do our experiences influence us and shape our identities?
    d. In what ways do "ghosts" haunt people?
    e. To what extent do choices have consequences?
    f. What is the most effective way to harness ambition?

    We have explored other questions as well, and you are free to address one of those for your project. Please run it by me first, though, so that I know what you are doing.

2. To explore the question you've chosen, select three texts we have read during class:
    a. *Trifles*
    b. "Story of an Hour"
    c. "The Handsomest Drowned Man in the World"
    d. "Araby"
    e. "The Use of Force"
    f. *Macbeth*
    g. *Interior Chinatown*
    h. "We Wear the Mask"
    i. "The Novel as a Function of American Democracy"
    j. Your Independent Novels

Figure 5.5a.   A Prompt for Self-Directed Literary Research.

3. Now that you have selected a question to explore and three texts you will use to explore that question, determine the route you will take. You might decide to do a traditional research essay, a creative project, or a combination of the two. In this phase of the project, you will have a lot of freedom to choose the route that works best to demonstrate your understanding. While I will show you some examples of past projects, I encourage you to draw on your own strengths and interests to design and create a project that shows your understanding. No matter what you do, however, you must demonstrate the following skills:

    a. Competent literary analysis that includes a strong, clear thesis; ample text evidence and insightful commentary; and at least one of the areas of "sophisticated," complex thinking as delineated in the AP scoring guideline.
    b. Effective use of MLA format. This is especially important when it comes to citing sources both within the text and in the Works Cited. If you do not include proper citations, I will not accept your project. Note: even creative projects require citations and a Works Cited. Similarly, plagiarism will result in a zero for the project.
    c. Ability to manage your time and meet deadlines. This is critical. Not only are you on a tight time schedule, but you are also part of a learning community in which everyone is balancing busy schedules and lives. Out of fairness to everyone, you must submit this project by the due date of January 20th.

While we will work on this project in class, especially during the week of the 16th-20th, you will also most likely need to budget time outside of class to finish this project in a way that meets your personal expectations as well as the expectations of this course. Remember to consult the AP scoring guide and scoring guide for this class (both in Teams), and to ask me any questions that might arise during your work. Feel free to ask for help before, during, or after class, or by email: erikp@spokaneschools.org.

Figure 5.5b.   A Prompt for Self-Directed Literary Research.

Another thing happens along the way: as I develop my skills as a listening partner, guide, and coach, I consider better ways to set up students for self-directed work. I am sure the assignment I gave this year will evolve into something quite different over the next few years. Even as I saw students work with ChatGPT during their projects, I found myself wondering how to guide them through that new reality of using the app as a tool instead of a replacement for their writing. Unanticipated questions came up on other topics, too, that challenged me to pause, reflect, and make notes for the future while also having to deal with their present needs.

In short, I still played a critical role in the process of helping students develop as self-directed learners. Anyone interested in trying this approach to learning, please be assured that your job will not go away as your students become better learners. If anything, you will become more deeply invested in crafting meaningful learning experiences and then supporting students as they engage in those experiences and develop as people of inquiry.

Structural Support

The individual support a teacher provides students going through this process perhaps goes further and means more than any specific program, framework, or how-to plan. Ideally, however, you can offer additional structural support to deal with the individual needs that will inevitably arise along the way of the learning journey. When I consider the responses of my colleagues to the questionnaire I sent them, for instance, I am deeply impressed with those who offer specific supporting structures to guide students and keep them on track during self-directed learning.

The work that has happened at St. Joseph High School in Edmonton, for example, among Brad Koshka, Ryan Feehan, and their colleagues (discussed in chapter 4) offers an especially promising model for how a school might establish specific support. Their plan for Guided Customized Learning (GCL)—named intentionally to clarify any of the confusion that frequently accompanies self-directed learning—includes what they describe as the four pillars of support for learning: Teacher Advisors, Personalize Scheduling, Customized Learning Experiences, and Authentic Assessment. As their program website (Guided Customized Learning, 2023) describes each of these pillars:

- **Teacher Advisor (TA):** Every student is assigned a TA who monitors their progress daily. Course Advisors are in constant contact with the TA, collaborating on how to best support each student. The TA helps the student plan their school day during morning and afternoon check-in. Students follow the schedule that has been approved by their TA.

- **Personalized Scheduling:** Students have scheduled seminars that they must attend. When not in a seminar, students work in the various learning floors and/or laboratories where they work individually, collaboratively, or have one-to-one instruction at guided help desks with subject area teachers.
- **Customized Learning Experiences:** Workshops offered during Guided Customized Learning blocks are created by Course Advisors based on the current needs of the students in their class. Students are encouraged to attend these workshops as a way of gaining an understanding of course material.
- **Authentic Assessment:** To prepare for seminars, students must access Google Classrooms and Moodle resources provided by the Course Advisors. When it is time for assessment, the Course Advisor will authorize a student's electronic test slip when the student has shown competency in the course outcomes. This is often completed during one-to-one meetings at the guided help desk. Students are given opportunities to challenge selected assessments to gain a full understanding of the curriculum.

Each of these pillars plays an important role in helping students to engage in the work of self-directed learning with the guidance offered along the way to sustain their work. It's a very well-thought-out structure, and I can only imagine that many schools interested in implementing this approach to learning system-wide would benefit from investigating the work at St. Joseph's.

I don't happen to teach in a school with such specific structures in place for self-directed learning; as a result, I, like many teachers, must do the best I can to collaborate with my colleagues to devise those supports for my students. Some of those supports have direct ramifications for my classes, and others simply do not. While my school has taken many steps to support students in a post-pandemic context (e.g., those discussed in chapter 4), we continue to work through different ideas and options that could help.

With that in mind, when I consider the four pillars at St. Joseph's, I wonder how I might implement them in my own class. Could I, for example, build in teacher-advisor time during class experiences? To some extent, I think that has happened over the years when I budget specific class time for students to work on projects. During those moments, I can meet with students to ask and answer their questions, offer additional resources, and act in ways to support their inquiry. Going forward, however, I would like to be even more intentional about designing and implementing that advising time to meet with students and help guide their progress.

Similarly, personalized scheduling might not happen on a large-scale basis at my school, but by designing choice learning for students and restructuring my class to function as a place of inquiry within those choices, I could be more intentional about supporting their independent work. Similar to the learning menus I have used in class or the learning stations that Ogata Sensei and Tamara Gower have used in their classes over the years, I can make connections with that pillar in place at St. Joseph's. As I write and reflect on these possibilities for my students, I imagine readers are doing the same thing: making connections and considering ways to innovate their own work. Teachers, of course, are learners, too, and their willingness to learn, revise, experiment, fail, and try again can go a long way toward helping their students.

The Customized Learning Experiences, too, can be part of a smaller class experience even if an entire school is not implementing such a system. I'm drawn to the idea of building specific moments to offer workshops to students on how to develop self-directedness, attack specific challenges in their work, or learn more about different aspects of inquiry. This strategy seems to align with a strategy recently delineated by McTighe and Tucker (2022): namely, to teach self-directed skills explicitly. If students do not know how to do this work, they will flounder without specific instruction and coaching on how to do it. Accordingly, McTighe and Tucker advise direct instruction on mapping key skills, breaking down complex skills into manageable components, and, drawing on Rosenshire (2012), providing both strategies and scaffolding tools to support learners during the process of acquiring, practicing, and applying their understanding of those skills (p. 60).

In some ways, the fourth pillar—authentic assessment—feels like it has been an established practice in my classes for years. That said, it doesn't necessarily look exactly the way St. Joseph describes it. I'm okay with that. For me, the goal is the authentic assessment itself. Can I implement it and track it in ways that work for my students? Absolutely. Am I open to adjust my assessment package to align more closely with the ideals of self-directed learning? I sure hope so. Do the assessments I have designed align with the targeted outcomes? Are they guided by essential questions that in turn guide students toward deeper thinking? While I still haven't found the perfect way to assess—let alone grade—student work, I believe I'm getting better at it each year. If I keep an open mind and learn from others, then I keep moving in the right direction for my practice which ultimately helps my students.

And just as I've been doing throughout this chapter, I will pause to invite readers to reflect (figure 5.6) on how they might currently connect with the four pillars in their own learning community as well as to consider how they might use them to initiate new strategies in their work.

Pillar	Connections—*How am I already doing this in my learning community?*	Considerations—*How might I incorporate this into my learning community?*
Teacher Advisors		
Personalized Scheduling		
Customized Learning Experiences		
Authentic Assessment		

Figure 5.6. The Four Pillars at Work.

SUMMARY

As educators build authentic relationships that address the social-emotional needs of their students, design strategic and academically purposeful experiences, and implement structural supports that serve as important scaffolds for learning, they establish the foundation for self-directed learning to happen in their learning communities. Whether that includes schoolwide implementation or individual classroom work, teachers can build on what they are already doing well while also learning from the real experiences of others who have tried and continue to try to help students develop as self-directed learners. Experimenting, revising, listening, and learning along the way can be just as important for teachers as it is for students.

Chapter 6

Coda

How important is this approach to learning? Does it stand as an ongoing luxury for some educators to try in their classes or for some schools to implement while others can afford to dismiss it as either frivolous, impractical, or simply too difficult? I hope that I have shown the relevance of self-directed learning in contemporary education, particularly in secondary schools. The research as well as the experiences of specific educators point overwhelmingly to the value of this approach no matter how challenging it is. While no one gets it perfect, they can continue to explore better ways to innovate and implement for the sake of developing self-directedness in their students.

To end this exploration into the approach, however, I would like to add that I do not see it as merely a fun, optional approach to learning but also an educational imperative in contemporary society. When I think of the emerging and ongoing needs of my students, particularly during the pandemic and post-pandemic contexts, I am convinced that they need to learn self-directedness more than ever.

Contemporary research (Dixon, 2016; Du Toit-Brits, 2021; Servant-Miklos and Noordegraaf-Eelens, 2021; and Tan, 2018) has pointed out both the challenges of existing paradigms and the need to forge new paths for students in order to develop not simply and individually as people of inquiry but also as transformative, contributing members of their communities. Now is the opportune time to explore new paradigms. This study has attempted to portray ways for teachers to address student needs that will prepare them to be independent learners. Building on that model, I would like to make one final move in the process: that is, delineating a model that shows how self-directedness can lead out from transformative principles and create learners equipped to contribute purposefully to their communities.

The work of partnering with students as people of inquiry might arguably trace its roots, at least in Western educational traditions, to Socrates. In more contemporary contexts, however, Freire's problem-posing approach serves as a solid foundation for this work. In saying this, I do not mean to exclude others or to suggest that Freire is the only one who has argued for this approach; at the same time, his dialectical approach continues to endure and influence contemporary researchers in relevant ways that offer immediacy to this exploration into self-directedness.

If we start with Freire's problem-posing as a base, then, we can see how contemporary research is able to build from that idea and lead students toward self-directedness not simply for their own enrichment but also for the purposeful transformation of their communities. Figure 6.1 attempts to depict that dynamic.

In this diagram, the dialectical approach for which Servant-Miklos and Noordegraaf-Eelens argued pairs with the idea of Tan's *Junzi* argument of the exemplary person and Du Toit-Brits' articulation of *Ubuntu*, respectively, to forge paths for students to engage in self-directed learning that will lead to meaningful contributions as community members who see themselves as connected, enriched people who then aim to contribute back to the communities that produced and nurtured them. With a coordinated approach along these lines, students stand more than a fighting chance to become not simply people of deep learning, but also people who reflect the qualities of self-directedness: not just goal-driven but also collaborative; not just communicatively adept but also self-aware (Du Toit-Brits, 2019, p. 16) and who move one step closer to realizing Freire's ideal of a "fuller humanity" (p. 21).

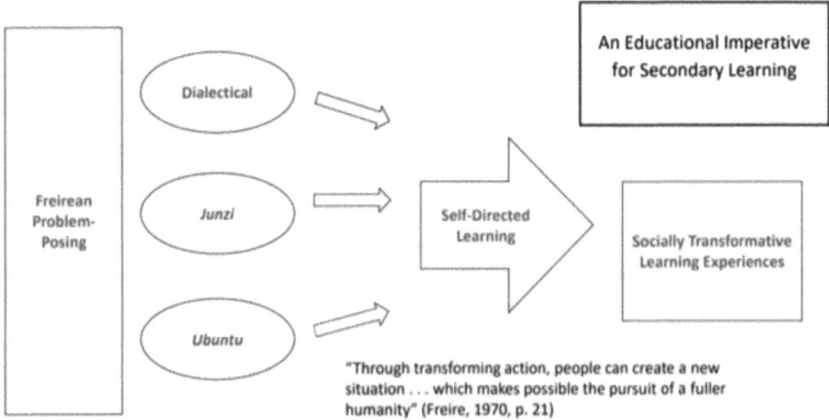

Figure 6.1. An Educational Imperative for Secondary Learning.

Learners nurtured in such a model, in fact, might be seen to exemplify the traits described by Broodryk (2006): that is, those who have experienced a successful education, meaning that they "live helpfully" and "grow into an endowed collective member who is compassionate, considerate, and understanding" (pp. 20–21). Given today's ongoing needs and contexts in society, including the many real challenges that schools face and the ways teachers must work within and around those contextual challenges, this model seems clearly to stand as an educational imperative for secondary teachers.

Furthermore, when considered in the context of Tabensky (2021), who articulated the ethical implications for learning, a transformative approach emerges as much more than a fun or optional add-on to education. The approach, despite the challenges of it and the nuanced demands of various academic disciplines, challenges educators to implement self-directedness as an ethical imperative.

According to Tabensky, "Genuine learning cannot happen without an agentic, indeed ethical, orientation towards learning" (p. 576). When paired with Broodryk's findings, Tabensky makes a compelling case, indeed, for forging pathways toward education as "finding our place" and "becoming" (pp. 568–569), which draws on the works of influential ethicists (Midgley, 1994; Foucault, 1997; and Rorty, 1999) to make what I hope is not too much of a leap to say: developing self-directed learners sets up educated people to make their communities better places to live.

But better, how? According to Tabensky, when educated people are not merely "self-directed" but rather use their learning "to expand outward ... to act as social beings able to embrace the lives of others in rich ways" (p. 572), then they can actually move closer to self-actualization that places them in the driver's seat of their learning not as "an optional extra" but as "a condition for living humanly" (pp. 574–576). In other words, the learning that expands outward beyond self-gratification or individual achievement and instead produces enrichments for the community, overall, is not a luxury but a crucial move toward living richer, fuller, and, yes, better lives.

The recent work of Bond et al. (2022) speaks further to this point and sets up a practical plan for teachers to help students not only develop their own critical thinking skills but also engage in socially transformative education. By guiding students through the process of identifying and describing a problem, listing options to solve the problem using research-based approaches, designing an action plan, and noticing the success of their problem-solving, teachers can foster routes that help students become more socially aware and transformative learners (p. 67).

And isn't that why many teachers entered education in the first place—to help others and serve their communities? Isn't this vocation, this calling, what drew many teachers to their work? What better way to do so, then, but to invest in students who will live and learn by taking ownership of their education and forge paths for themselves, and, ideally, paths that help others? The task is far from easy; in fact, it seems to get increasingly difficult each year. Obstacles and challenges arise from numerous sources in seemingly endless waves that could (and do) cause disheartened educators to throw up their hands and quit.

I'd offer, though, that after nearly thirty years as a classroom teacher, I see these challenges as more compelling than ever to keep going, to invest in students, and to invest in self-directed learning. The work to move students toward transformative inquiry is anything but easy. Investing in authentic relationships, designing purposeful learning experiences, and implementing sustainable structures of support are not easy challenges. Instead, they often turn out to be messy, challenging, and complex. What works for one class doesn't work for another; what works for one school might very well not work for another. We try, though, and we stumble, regroup, and try again. We do this knowing that, while difficult, these tasks are also completely worth the effort, as I hope the following anecdote illustrates.

Recently, many of my tenth graders struggled mightily with an assessment over the Greek tragedy *Antigone*. That tenth graders would not have a natural interest in Sophoclean drama should surprise no one (especially someone who has taught it as long as I have); that they should have struggled to the extent that they did with this quiz absolutely floored me. My co-teacher and I had worked hard to design an interactive, differentiated approach to exploring the play and had used this particular exam for several years as part of our overall assessment package for the unit. Students in previous years had by and large done well on it and used it, along with an accompanying creative project that incorporates many self-directed options, to demonstrate their understanding of the play's characters, plot, and themes. This year, however, something went awry with the exam as too many students failed who had seemed to understand the play during discussions and other parts of the unit.

Instead of throwing our hands up in despair, denouncing the laziness of *kids these days*, or beating ourselves up for failing as teachers (all of which I've done in the past and will probably do again in the future at some point), we remembered the advice of Dixon (2016) to listen to students. We explained to the class that the results—while positive for many—concerned us for quite a few students in each class period. We asked them three questions to help us understand what, from their perspective, had gone wrong with the test.

First, we asked them by way of multiple choice to identify the aspects of the test that proved so challenging: format, difficulty, outside distractions, didn't study, or others. Among the three class periods, "outside distractions" came in as the top vote getter. "Didn't study" received the next highest number of votes. In the "other" category, most students responded by saying the test was not difficult for them.

Second, we asked students to describe a way to demonstrate their understanding in a more personalized, self-directed way. Again, many said the test format was fine; others, however, described a range of assessment options consistent with some of the other performance tasks they had done throughout the year.

Third, we asked them to re-affirm their basic understanding of the play by identifying the main characters, summarizing the plot, and discussing one theme. The intention here was to give them a "win" coming out of the reflection and to identify exactly what they could recall off the top of their head about the play.

From there, we established several learning options for revision. For those students who performed well on the original test, time would be available to them to work on their forthcoming independent reading projects. For students who struggled only with certain parts of the test, a re-do opportunity would be available, as would the option of doing a more personalized assessment. Students who did not pass the initial exam would re-do parts that did not go well and do a personalized assessment.

On the one hand, we could have simply chalked this up to an exam failure for many, scolded them for not being more diligent, and moved on with class. On the other hand, those responses did not feel consistent with the occasion or, more significantly, our mission as educators. By pausing, listening to students, and re-thinking ways to guide them to success, what we saw that week was an expression of self-directedness. Structures helped students show their understanding as we placed them in the driver's seat of their learning. Social-emotional learning helped many students as we met with them individually to listen and help them reflect and re-focus their efforts. Intentionality led to a more purposeful array of learning experiences.

As a result, we saw students not only improve their scores but also—and perhaps more importantly—communicate their understanding in ways that played to their strengths, helped them make more authentic connections with the text, and empowered them to make decisions for their own learning. For some of those students, many with staggering social-emotional needs, this stood as a significant step toward autonomy and self-directedness. For my co-teacher and me, it was an important reminder to value the human spirit of the education process and the needs of the whole child. While this process may have taken some extra time and patience, it resonated with our professional and personal values as teachers and learners. The reality is that learning does not always come on a straight, level path, either in school or in life. Likewise, school is not simply an academic clearing house, but rather a living, breathing community in which teachers and students build strategies together to grow as people of inquiry.

References

Abdullah, M. (2001). Self-directed learning. Accessed 18 November 2020, from http://files.eric. ed.gov/fulltext/ED459458.pdf.

Battelle for Kids. (2019). Framework for 21st-centurty learning definitions: Partnership for 21st-century learning. www.battelleforkids.org/networks/p21

Billups, F. (2021). *Qualitative data collection tools: Design, development, and applications.* Los Angeles, CA: Sage.

Boaler, J. (2002). *Experiencing school mathematics: Traditional and reform approaches to teaching and their impact on student learning* (Rev. and exp. ed.). Lawrence Erlbaum Associates.

Bond, L., Fullmer, L., Elias, M., & Cohen, R. (2022). Creating a powerful PLAN. *Educational Leadership, 80*(3), 66–72.

Brandt, C. (2020). *Measuring student success skills: A review of the literature on self-directed learning.* www.ncia.org

Broodryk, J. (2006). Ubuntu African life coping skills: Theory and practice, in recreating linkages between theory and praxis in educational leadership. *The Commonwealth Council for Educational Administration and Management (CCEAM) Conference*, Nicosia, Cyprus, October 12–17, 13–22.

Brown, D. (2022). Florida will have a new statewide assessment system but hurdles lie ahead. *Florida Phoenix*, March 15. https://floridaphoenix.com/2022/03/15/fl-will-have-a-new-statewide-assessment-system-but-hurdles-lie-ahead/

Burton, R. (1982). Anatomy of melancholy. In A. Witherspoon & F. Warnke (Eds.), *Seventeenth-century prose and poetry* (2nd ed., p. 136). Harcourt Brace Jovanovich College Publishers. (original work published 1621)

Chiu, D. (2022, May 4). Jazz bassist Ron Carter on his iconic career ahead of 85th birthday concert at Carnegie Hall. *Forbes.* https://www.forbes.com/sites/davidchiu/2022/05/04/jazz-bassist-ron-carter-on-his-iconic-career-ahead-of-85th-birthday-concert-at-carnegie-hall/?sh=2e5a482879ba

Costa, A., & Kallick, B. (2004). *Assessment strategies for self-directed learners.* Thousand Oaks, CA: Corwin.

Czarnecki, S. (2023). Labor-based grading: A new ethic for writing feedback. *English Journal, 112*(6), 56–62.

DeBarger, A. (2021). What if classrooms were rooted in care? *Hewlett Foundation*, February 3. https://hewlett.org/what-if-classrooms-were-rooted-in-care/

Dintersmith, T. (2018). *What schools could be: Insights and inspiration from teachers across America*. Princeton: Princeton University Press.

Dixon, B. (2016). *The end of school as we know it*. Bloomington, IN: Solution Tree.

Du Toit-Brits, C. (2019). A focus on self-directed learning: The role that educators' expectations play in the enhancement of students' self-directedness. *South African Journal of Education, 39*(2), 1–11.

Du Toit-Brits, C. (2021). The influence of the learning environment on promoting self-directed learning, in E. Mentz, D. Laubscher, & J. Olivier (Eds.), *Self-directed learning: An imperative for education in a complex society* (NWU Self-Directed Learning Series Volume 6, pp. 25–44). Cape Town: AOSIS. https://doi.org/10.4102/aosis.2021.BK279.02

Ellison, T. (2017). Digital participation, agency, and choice: An African American youth's digital storytelling about Minecraft. *JAAL, 61*(1), 25–35.

Ertmer, P.A.. & Newby, T.J. (1996). The expert learner: Strategic, self-regulated and reflective. *Instructional Science, 24*(1), 1–24. https://doi.org/10.1007/BF00156001

Evans, B. (1959). [Liner Notes]. In *Kind of Blue*. Columbia.

Ferris High School Climate Survey. (2020). Spokane Public Schools. Panorama Education. www.panoramaed.com

Ford, R. (2021). Adventures in gaming and personalized learning: A case study in genre-based course design. *ELQ, 43*(3), 7–12.

Foucault, M. (1997). The ethics of the concern of the self as a practice of freedom. In P. Rabinow (Ed.), *The essential works of Michel Foucault: Subjectivity and truth* (vol. 1). New York: The New Press.

Freire, P. (1970). *Pedagogy of the oppressed* (M. Bergman Ramos, Trans.). London: Penguin Books.

Friedman, S. (2014). *Total leadership: Be a better leader, have a richer life*. Harvard Business Review Press.

Fullan, M., Quinn, J., Drummy, M., & Gardner, M. (2020). Education reimagined: The future of learning. *New pedagogies for deep learning and Microsoft education*. http://aka.ms/HybridLearningPaper

Gray, P. (2020a). *Mother nature's pedagogy: Biological foundations for children's self-directed education*. Alliance for Self-Directed Education.

Gray, P. (2020b). *Evidence that self-directed education works*. Alliance for Self-Directed Education.

Grow, G. (1991). Teaching learners to be self-directed. *Adult Education Quarterly, 41*(3), 125–149.

Guglielmino, L.M. (2013). The case for promoting self-directed learning in formal educational institutions. *South African Education Journal, 10*(2), 1–18.

Guided Customed Learning (2023). Edmonton Catholic Schools. https://www.ecsd.net/guided-customized-learning-gcl-

Hancock, L. (2011). Why are Finland's schools so successful? *Smithsonian Magazine*, September. https://www.smithsonianmag.com/innovation/why-are-finlands-schools-successful-49859555/

Heifetz, R., Grashow, A., & Linksy, M. (2009). *The practice of adaptive leadership: Tools and tactics for changing your organization and the world*. Harvard Business Review Press.

Jackson, A. (2016). Finland has one of the world's best education systems. Here's how it compares to the US. *World Economic Forum*, November 21. https://www.weforum.org/agenda/2016/11/finland-has-one-of-the-worlds-best-education-systems-four-ways-it-beats-the-us

Jenson, J., & Droumeva, M. (2017). Revisiting the media generation. *E-learning & Digital Media, 14*(4), 212–225.

Joel E. Ferris High School: 2019 Profile File. (2019). https://www.spokaneschools.org/site/handlers/filedownload.ashx?moduleinstanceid=15180&dataid=13909&FileName=ferris-profile-2019.pdf

Kahn, S., Hussain, I., ud Din, M., Ahmed, M., & Ahmed, S. (2012). Self-directed learning in mathematics at the secondary level. *Academic Research International, 2*(2): 168–171.

Kallick, B., & Zmuda, A. (2017). *Students at the center: Personalized learning with habits of mind*. Alexandria, VA: ASCD.

Knowles, M. (1975). *Self-directed learning: A guide for learners and teachers*. Englewood Cliffs: Prentice Hall/Cambridge.

Learning menus: *textbooks à la carte*. National History Education Clearing House. https://teachinghistory.org/best-practices/teaching-with-textbooks/25584

Leavy, P. (2017). *Research design: Quantitative, qualitative, mixed methods, arts-based, and community-based participatory research approaches*. New York: The Guilford Press.

Lee, V.E., Smith, J.B., Perry, T.E., & Smylie, M.A. (1999). Social support, academic press, and student achievement: A view from the middle grades in Chicago. Retrieved from https://ccsr.uchicgao.edu/sites/default/files/publications/p0e01.pdf

Liden, R., Wayne, S., Zhao, H., & Henderson, D. (2008). Servant leadership: Development of a multidimensional measure and multi-level assessment. *The Leadership Quarterly, 19*(2), 161–177. https://doi.org/10.1016/j.leaqua.2008.01.006.

Liljedahl, P. (2021). *Building thinking classrooms in mathematics: 14 teaching practices for enhancing learning*. Thousand Oaks, CA: Corwin.

Lounsbury, J.W., Jacob, J.J., Park, S., Gibson, L.W., & Smith, R. (2009). An investigation on the construct validity of the personality trait of self-directed learning, *Learning and Individual Differences, 19*(4), 411–418. https://doi.org/10.1016/j.lindif.2009.03.001

Martirena, C. (2022). Responding to the needs of every young learner. *Edutopia*, November 23.

McCourt, F. (2005). *Teacher man*. New York: Scribner.

McLaughlin, M., & Talbert, J. (1993). Introduction: New visions for teaching. In D. Cohen, M. McLaughlin, & J. Talbert (Eds.), *Teaching for understanding* (p. 1). San Francisco: Jossey Bass.

McTighe, J., Silver, H., & Perini, M. (2020). *Deep learning is doable: Five strategies for supporting deep learning in virtual environments.* White Paper.

McTighe, J., & Tucker, C. (2022). Developing self-directed learners by design. *Educational Leadership, 80*(3), 58–64.

Mehta, J., & Fine, S. (2019). *In search of deeper learning: The quest to remake the American high school.* Cambridge, MA: Harvard University Press.

Mentz, E. (2021). Self-directed learning: Putting the "self" in learning. *SDL Research Unit Booklet*, North-West University. https://nextcloud.nwu.ac.za/index.php/s/QTHiRDNKrq3KrFd

Mentz, E., Laubscher, D., & Olivier, J., eds. (2021). *Self-directed learning: An imperative for education in a complex society.* Cape Town: AOSIS.

Merriam, S. (2017). Adult learning theory: Evolution and future directions. *PAACE Journal of Lifelong Learning, 26*, 21–37.

Meyer, D. (2010). Math class needs a makeover. TEDxNYED. https://www.ted.com/talks/dan_meyer_math_class_needs_a_makeover/transcript

Meyer, D. (2023). dy/dan. https://blog.mrmeyer.com/

Microsoft. (2020). *The class of 2030 and life-ready learning: The technology imperative, a summary report.* Microsoft.

Midgley, M. (1994). *The ethical primate: Humans, freedom and morality.* London: Routledge.

Mullen, G. (2020). *Creating a self-directed learning environment: Standards-based and social-emotional learning.* Thousand Oaks, CA: Corwin.

Pane, J., et al. (2017). Informing progress: Insights on personalized learning implementation and effects. *Gates Foundation.* https://doi.org/10.7249/RR2042

Perkins, D. (2020). Why creating a culture of inquiry is so important. *Teach Thought*, January 15. https://www.teachthought.com/pedagogy/culture-of-inquiry/

Pope, D. (2001). *"Doing school": How we are creating a generation of stressed out, materialistic, and miseducated students.* New Haven, CT: Yale University Press.

Powell, E. (2021, April 1). Three pandemic lessons for teachers to carry forward. *ASCD Inservice.* https://inservice.ascd.org/three-pandemic-lessons-to-carry-forward/

Robinson, J., & Persky, A. (2020). Developing self-directed learners. *American Journal of Pharmaceutical Education, 84*(3), 292–296.

Rorty, R. (1999). Education as socialization and as individuation. In R. Rorty (Ed.), *Philosophy and social hope.* New York: Penguin Books, 114–126.

Rosenshire, B. (2012). Principles of instruction: Research-based strategies that all teachers should know. *American Educator, 36*(1), 12–39.

Rouse, T. (2021). *Finding refuge: Real-life immigration stories from young people.* Zest Books.

Rushdie, S. (1989). *Satanic Verses.* Dover, DE: The Consortium.

Salina, C., Girtz, S., & Eppinga, J. (2016). *Powerless to powerful: Leadership for school change*. Lanham, MD: Rowman & Littlefield.

Samson, D.J. (2013). How self-directed learning works. *Obooko*. Accessed 07 June 2020, from http:// www.obooko.com/obooko_business/bookpages/business/free%20ebook-self-directedlearning-samson-bus0024.

Savransky, B. (2021). "A very McCarthyism feel": Idaho teachers say indoctrination task force stokes fear. *Education Week*, July 29. https://www.edweek.org/policy-politics/a-very-mccarthyism-feel-idaho-teachers-say-indoctrination-task-force-stokes-fear/2021/07

Schmoker, M. (2010). When pedagogic fads trump priorities. *Education Week*, September 27. https://www.edweek.org/teaching-learning/opinion-when-pedagogic-fads-trump-priorities/2010/09

Schnall, P., Prod. and Dir. (2022). *Ron Carter: Finding the right notes*. New York: Partisan Pictures.

Seif, E. (2021). *Teaching for lifelong learning: How to prepare students for a changing world*. Bloomington, IN: Solution Tree.

Sendjaya, S., & Sarros, J.C. (2002). Servant leadership: Its origin, development, and application in organizations. *Journal of Leadership and Organization Studies*, 9, 57–64. https://doi.org/10.1177/107179190200900205

Serrat, O. (2017). *Knowledge solutions*. Singapore: Singer.

Servant-Miklos, V., & Noordegraaf-Eelens, L. (2021). Toward social-transformative education: An ontological critique of self-directed learning. *Critical Studies in Education*, 62(2), 147–163. https://doi.org/10.1080/17508487.2019.1577284

Sheridan, K. (2022). "We are not being indoctrinated." Students, teachers say Florida's new education laws stifle schools. *WUSF Public Media*. https://wusfnews.wusf.usf.edu/education/2022-08-25/students-teachers-florida-new-education-laws-stifle-schools

Skeeters, K., et al. (2016). Top 5 reasons we love giving students choice in reading. *English Leadership Quarterly*, February, 6–7.

Spokane Public Schools. (2021, July 12). Strategic plan: Guiding principles. https://www.spokaneschools.org/Page/1650

Sumantri, M., & Satriani, R. (2016). The effect of formative testing and self-directed learning on mathematics learning outcomes. *International Electronic Journal of Elementary Education*, 8(3), 507–524.

Tabensky, P. (2021). Ethics and education as practices of freedom. *Educational Philosophy and Theory*, 53(6), 568–577.

Tan, C. (2018). Wither teacher-directed learning?: Freirean and Confucian thoughts. *The Educational Forum*, 82(4), 461–474. https://doi.org/10.1080/00131725.2018.1475713

Tchudi, S., ed. (1996). *Alternatives to grading student writing*. Urbana, IL: NCTE.

Tomlinson, C., & McTighe, J. (2006). *Integrating differentiated instruction and understanding by design*. Alexandria, VA: ASCD.

Tredoux, C. (2012). The potential of a learning management system to enhance self-directed learning, MEd dissertation, North-West University.

Wehmayer, M., & Yong, Z. (2020). *Teaching students to become self-directed learners*. Alexandria, VA: ASCD.

Weselby, C. (2022). What is differentiated instruction? Examples of how to differentiate instruction in the classroom. *Resilient Educator*, November 8. https://resilienteducator.com/classroom-resources/examples-of-differentiated-instruction/

Whitehead, A. (1929). *The aims of education and other essays*. New York: Macmillan.

Wiggins, G., & McTighe, J. (1998). *Understanding by design*. Alexandria, VA: ASCD.

Wiggins, G., & McTighe, J. (2004). *Understanding by design professional development workbook*. Alexandria, VA: ASCD.

Will, M. (2018). To make ends meet, 1 in 5 teachers have second jobs. *Education Week*, June 19. https://www.edweek.org/leadership/to-make-ends-meet-1-in-5-teachers-have-second-jobs/2018/06

Zerwin, S. (2020). *Point-less: An English teacher's guide to more meaningful grading*. Portsmouth, NH: Heinemann.

Index

Note: Page locators in italics refer to figures.

academic strategy, 66–73
Achebe, Chinua, 21
Advanced Placement English Literature and Composition, 37
Alliance for Self-Directed Education, 5
Antigone, 80
Association of Supervision and Curriculum Development (ASCD), 37, 44
authentic assessment, 74, 75, *76*
authentic relationships, 62–66, *64*

backward design, 18–19, 68
banking approach, 54
bell-to-bell instruction, 59
big ideas, 9, 19, 20, 52
Boaler, J., 53
Bond, L., 79
Brandt, C., 7
Broodryk, J., 79
bubbles, 47, 48

Canada, 6, 41, 46
Carnegie Unit model, 13
Carter, Ron, 16, 17, 32
Catholic school, Chicago, 46
ChatGPT, 71, 73

Christa McAuliffe Excellence in Teacher Education Award, 44
classroom, 3, 5, 17, 43, 47, 62; activities, 44; community, 49; environment, 34; teachers, 6, 20, 80; wall, 3, 58
cognitive skills, 9
collaborative response model, 52, 58
community-building activity, 59, 64
Community Resilience Initiative, 62
comprehensive input strategy, 44
Confucian concept, 8
contemporary research, 11, 48, 77, 78
Cortner, Diane, 56
Course Advisor, 73, 74
COVID-19 pandemic, 1, 10, 54
critical thinking, 10, 79
The Crucible, 63
cultural-historical psychology, 29, 32
customized learning experiences, 74, 75, *76*

data analysis, 47–48
data collection, 47–48
Davis, Miles, 16, 17, 32
DeBarger, A., 62
deep learning, 9, 10, 20, 46, 78

Development Committee for English Literature and Composition, 47
dialectical approach, 29, 78
differentiated instruction, 20–26, 52
differentiated learning, 56
Dixon, B., 4, 80
Droumeva, M., 70
Du Toit-Brits, C., 8, 33, 78

educational imperative, secondary learning, 78, 78
Educational Testing Services, 37
educators, 2, 7, 37, 46, 55, 61, 76; Big ideas, 19; from Canada, 41; discernment of, 17; guide students, 29; learning experiences, 8; in State of Washington, 1; in student-centered learning, 29; survey, 3
English Language Arts, 21
English Literature and Composition Committee, 47
Evans, Bill, 16

Feehan, Ryan, 46, 49–51, 73
Ferris, 37, 39–41, 53, 67
Ferris participants: Ashley Jones, 43, 50, 51, 54, 55, 58; Darci Hastings, 43, 49, 53, 56, 57, 59, 67; Emily Torres, 44–45, 49–51, 56, 62, 63; James Noble, 44, 50, 53–55, 58; Karissa Jacobson, 23, 43, 49, 50, 52, 55, 56, 59, 65; Ogata Sensei, 44, 50, 51, 54, 67, 75; Tamara Gower, 42–43, 49, 51, 55, 67, 75; Tom Rye, 44, 49, 51–53, 61
Fine, S., 4, 10, 45, 52, 53, 63
Finland, 64, 65
Finnish model, 64
frameworks, 9, 16–18; Differentiated Instruction, 20–26; multi-tiered framework, 49; Understanding by Design. *See* Understanding by Design
Freire, P., 3, 4, 8, 54, 78
Freirean-Vygotskian dialectal model, 28

Friedman, S., 38
Fulbright Teacher Exchange, Argentina, 42
Fullan, M., 4
fuller humanity, 78

Galvez, Adam, 46, 50, 51, 54, 58, 59
Gates Foundation, 8
GCL. *See* Guided Customized Learning (GCL)
Gonzaga University, 43, 44
Gower, Tamara, 42–43, 49, 51, 55, 67, 75
Gradgrind, Thomas, 59
Gray, P., 5
Guided Customized Learning (GCL), 73

Hancock, Herbie, 16
Harkness Method, 47, 50, 54, 58, 67
Hastings, Darci, 43, 49, 53, 56, 57, 59, 67
Heifetz, R., 34, 35
Heikkinen, Timo, 65
Hewlett Foundation, 10
Hunter, Enithie, 46–47, 50, 53, 54, 58, 67

Individualized Education Plans (IEPs), 21
innovation, 16, 18, 43, 44
International Science and Engineering Fair (ISEF), 56

Jacobson, Karissa, 23, 43, 49, 50, 52, 55, 56, 59, 65
Jay McTighe & Associates, 37
jazz, 16, 17
Jenson, J., 70
Joel E. Ferris High School. *See* Ferris
Jones, Ashley, 43, 50, 51, 54, 55, 58
Jooma, Minaz Dr., 47, 49, 54, 66
junzi, 8, 78

Kallick, B., 5
Kind of Blue, 16
Knowles, M., 3, 7, 9, 10, 41, 52, 71
Koshka, Brad, 46, 50–52, 58, 73

learning community, 21, 38–42, 61, 64, 75
lifelong learning, 9, 10, 31, 44
Liljedahl, P., 53
long-term transformation, 29

McCourt, F., 13
McLaughlin, M., 3
McTighe, J., 3, 5, 9, 20, 21, 37, 68, 75
McTighe & Associates, 44
Mehta, J., 4, 10, 45, 46, 52, 53, 63
Meyer, D., 13, 53
Microsoft (2020), 9
Ministry of Education and Culture, 65
Montessori class, 67
multi-tiered framework, 49

The Netherlands, 28
New York City, 13, 14
Noble, James, 44, 50, 53–55, 58
non-Ferris participants: Adam Galvez, 46, 50, 51, 54, 58, 59; Brad Koshka, 46, 50–52, 58, 73; Dr. Minaz Jooma, 47, 49, 54, 66; Enithie Hunter, 46–47, 50, 53, 54, 58, 67; Jim Wickes, 47, 50, 52; Ryan Feehan, 46, 49–51, 73
Noordegraaf-Eelens, L., 28–30, 77–78
North-West University, 5, 32
"Now what?," 30–35, *31*, 38

O'Dell, John, 40
Ogata, Shiho, 44, 50, 51, 54, 67, 75
Ogata Sensei. *See* Ogata, Shiho
Okonkwo, 22

Pane, J., 8
Perkins, D., 5
personalized learning, 8, 9, 54
personalized scheduling, 74, *76*
PLTW. *See* Project Lead the Way (PLTW)
Pope, D., 3
post-pandemic: academic work, 69, *69*; context, 41, 69, 74; protocol, 6, 17, 57
post-Rogerian educational system, 32

problem-posing approach, 4, 8, 22, 29, 32, 78
problem-solving skill, 10
Programme for International Student Assessment, 66
Project Lead the Way (PLTW), 43, 49, 53, 57, 67

qualitative analysis, 41, 60
Quirkos, 47

ren, 8
Rogerian educational system, 32
Rogerian learning theory, 29
Rosenshire, B., 75
RPG, 22
Rushdie, S., 1
Rye, Tom, 44, 49, 51–53, 61

Sahlberg, Pasi, 65
Salina, C., 59
Satanic Verses, 1
scaffolding, 49, 50, 60, 75
Seif, E., 4, 10
self-actualization, 79
self-directed learning, 3, 4, 6–11, 41; academic strategy, 66–73; authentic relationships, 62–66, *64*; challenges, 41, 42, 51–55, 80; in contemporary education, 77; design and implement, 48–50, *49*; design template, *67*, 68; Differentiated Instruction, 20–26; four pillars, 73–74, *76*; Harkness Method, 54; implications, 57–60; importance, 15–17; learn about ourselves and school culture, 55–57; learning community, 38–42; "Now what?," 30–35, *31*, 38; obstacles, 41, 42, 51–55, 80; Research Unit, South Africa, 32; Rogerian conceptualization, 28; structural support, 73–76; too time-consuming, 34; *ubuntu*, 32–34; Understanding by Design. *See* Understanding by Design; "Yeah, but," 28–30, *31*. *See also individual entries*

Self-Directed Literary Research, 71, *72*
self-efficacy, 9
Servant-Miklos, V., 28–30, 77–78
shared qualities, 45–46
social-emotional learning, 25, 59, 81
Socrates, 78
South African university, 8
status quo, 34
St. Joseph High School, Edmonton, 73–75
structural support, 73–76
students, 5, 14, 21, 25–26, 51, 53, 56, 59, 66, 67, 74, 81; centered instruction, 9; in dialectal exploration, 29; at Ferris, 39; guiding toward self-reflection, 29; in post-pandemic academic work, 69, *69*; in RPG, 22; social-emotional needs of, 62; at South African university, 8; during trajectory-shifting, 2

TA. *See* Teacher Advisor (TA)
Tabensky, P., 79
Talbert, J., 3
Tan, C., 8, 78
Task Verification, 51
Teacher Advisor (TA), 73, *76*
teachers, 14, 18, 19, 22, 29, 30, 53, 59, 63, 68, 79; efforts, 5; in Finland, 65; headaches for teachers, 54; in Massachusetts, 15; in New York City public school, 13
technical changes, 35

TED talk, 13
textbook-based curriculum, 4, 5
Things Fall Apart (Achebe), 21
Tomlinson, C., 20, 21
Torres, Emily, 44–45, 49–51, 56, 62, 63
trajectory-shifting: COVID-19 pandemic, 1; educators survey, 3; novel, 1; students need during, 2
Tucker, C., 75
typical approaches, 39

ubuntu, 32–34, 64, 78
Understanding by Design (UbD), 5; backward design, 18–19; Big ideas, 19; essential question, 19–20; performance tasks, 20
United States, 3, 4, 6, 9, 13, 14, 41, 44–46, 52, 66

Vygotsky's approach, 29

Washington State Capitol, 56
Wehmeyer, M., 30
Whitehead, A., 3, 4
Wickes, Jim, 47, 50, 52
Wiggins, G., 3, 9, 68
World Language Department, 67

"Yeah, but," 28–30, *31*

Zhao, Y., 30
Zmuda, A., 5

About the Author

Since **Erik N. Powell** began teaching in 1994, he has enjoyed working with other educators to design and implement engaging, challenging, and meaningful learning experiences for students. While he has taught at both the high school and college levels, he has spent most of his career at Joel E. Ferris High School in Spokane where he teaches English and, occasionally, French. Additionally, as a consultant for both ASCD and Jay McTighe & Associates, he has provided professional development across the United States by collaborating with schools and districts to help them reach their professional goals. His work in the classroom was featured in *Moving Forward with Understanding by Design* (2007), and he has been a guest blogger for ASCD's In-Service (2021).

Erik's work with the College Board, moreover, includes assessing and aligning standards for pre-AP and AP English, co-authoring materials for College Ed (2010), and serving as co-chair for the AP English Literature and Composition Development Committee. He edited and co-authored the *Curriculum Module Developing Analytical Skills through Poetry* (2012) and has served as an item writer for the AP English Literature and Composition exam. Much of his recent work has focused on the challenges educators face while trying to implement self-directed learning experiences in their classes. Erik earned his doctorate in educational leadership from Gonzaga University.

www.ingramcontent.com/pod-product-compliance
Lightning Source LLC
Chambersburg PA
CBHW030147240426
43672CB00005B/311